PRAISE FOR
Feral Magick

"Was he raised by wolves? Author Denny Sargent reminds us in *Feral Magick* that a magician needs to nourish and honor their wild side. We magicians are human, but we are also animal, our most positive side. Strip away restrictive conditions, be 'unfettered, nature orientated, free of captivity and, most of all, wild.' This type of spirited, free-form shamanism must become part of our basic skill set. This book represents the spirit of the old Neopagan mantra: 'be wild, be free, be true to me.' This, according to the author, is the way of all natural Pagans, and what he promulgates and teaches in this lovely book."
—Mogg Morgan, founder of Mandrake of Oxford

"At a time when so many of us feel that we are disconnected from the rest of Nature, *Feral Magick* offers a way of rewilding ourselves in body and spirit. By opening ourselves to an animistic worldview, we are invited to return to who and what we once were—and never really ceased to be."
—Lupa, creator of *The Tarot of Bones* deck and book

"A writer, teacher, and practitioner of esoteric traditions since the seventies, Denny Sargent conveys his scholarship and experience through his passion for animism and wildness. *Feral Magick* is a book that will awaken your primal self and help you reclaim your place in nature: a reminder that we are feral, a howling call from the bowels of freedom itself."
—André Consciência, author of *A Guide to the Elementals* and other books

"*Feral Magick* is a call to unshackle the domesticated mind and awaken the wild intelligence within. Denny Sargent weaves a path of initiation that is as inevitable as it is transformational— reminding us that true power is not taken but embodied. Read it and remember what you were before the world told you otherwise."
—Entelecheia, author of *Erotic Liberation* and *The Adventures of a God*

"Ever wonder why the earliest systems of magick, shamanism, and witchcraft are so effective despite not utilizing grimoires? These systems grew out of animism—an understanding that everything is alive, and the world is full of nature spirits who can guide those who are open to them. So many live in urban centers totally divorced from nature and their own primal animal selves. Paganism is very earth-based or nature-oriented, but for many, this is limited to harmonizing with the harvest calendar and working the Wheel of the Year. While a step in the right direction, it stops well short of what can be achieved. *Feral* or *wild* magick is an escape from the "domestication" of the modern world, so as to revert to a wild condition. The process utilizes techniques to leave behind the ego and assume the primal consciousness of the animal self in order to communicate and bond with nature spirits and their powers. This results in a free-flowing intuitive practice standing in stark contrast to rigid grimoire-based workings. This will be an end in itself for some, while for others it will be something to be incorporated to amplify existing practices."

—Tony Mierzwicki, author of *Hellenismos: Practicing Greek Polytheism Today*

"Denny Sargent's *Feral Magick* might just be the most important book you read this year. As our present human society continues to be subsumed into the more dystopian developments of its ever-unfurling technocracy, *Feral Magick* offers a complete course in liberation from artifice and oppression, connecting the reader, through a series of practical exercises, to a world more thrilling, expansive, and teeming with life and soul than could be guessed.

"Denny offers everything required to begin right now, today, on the path of neo-animism, a worldview in which, quite literally, everything is alive and charged with spirit. Within these pages you'll find clear direction as to how you can encounter real spirit guides, often found flying, hopping, or prowling about the periphery of one's leash. If such a tether has kept you from breaking free and truly running wild in a living landscape, if you wish to unveil and dance with the depths of your very being, *Feral Magick* provides the tools and points the way. Should you answer the call and put into practice what Denny has put onto paper, you may be assured that you won't see the world—or yourself—the same way again!"

—Kyle Fite, artist and author of *Hoodoo Pilot,*
Advent of the Space Master, and *Beyond the Golden Omen*

"This book points to the experience of something deeply embedded in our being, in our DNA. There is a wildness that simmers, bubbling within all of us. *Feral Magick* stretches into that wildness, birthing new and intimate relationships with nature. Our world grows larger as we 'step sideways' into nature, less dependent on an enculturated selectivity, more inclusive and open to wonder. *Feral Magick* focuses on our senses and clearly describes how, through their extension, we can open to the abundant spirited forms of life that surround us. Once open, we can ride our senses to directly experience the nature spirits. Instinct, intuition, and insight provide sure guides in this undertaking. The reader is then well equipped to work with the more complex animal spirits, spirit-kin, and to feel the joy in finding their personal spirit-kin animal. Neo-animism, the experiential basis of Denny's work, invites the reader to enter a larger world. A world in which the reader is no longer isolated, no longer experiencing the loneliness engendered by a separation from the loving, beating heart of nature. *Feral Magick* is an invitation to freedom. It is a call, not to 'grow up' but to 'grow out,' to open to all of the life that surrounds us with the senses of a child. To experience our 'primal spirit' radiating as pure love and a greatness of heart."

—Dr. Louie Martinié, cofounder of Black Moon Publishing

FERAL MAGICK

Unleash Your Inner Animal Self

DENNY SARGENT

WEISER BOOKS

This edition first published in 2025 by Weiser Books, an imprint of
Red Wheel/Weiser, LLC
With offices at:
65 Parker Street, Suite 7
Newburyport, MA 01950
www.redwheelweiser.com

Copyright © 2025 by Denny Sargent
All rights reserved. No part of this publication may be reproduced or transmitted in any form or by any means, electronic or mechanical, including photocopying, recording, or by any information storage and retrieval system, nor used in any manner for purposes of training artificial intelligence (AI) technologies to generate text or imagery, including technologies that are capable of generating works in the same style or genre, without permission in writing from Red Wheel/Weiser, LLC. Reviewers may quote brief passages.

ISBN: 978-1-57863-851-2
Library of Congress Cataloging-in-Publication Data available upon request.

Cover design by Sky Peck Design
Interior images by Cosmic Store/Creative Market, iStock
Interior by Brittany Craig
Typeset in Arno Pro

Printed in the United States of America
IBI
10 9 8 7 6 5 4 3 2 1

DEDICATION

This book is dedicated to all the shamans I have met, worked with, and known and who helped opened their Otherworld to me. They and others showed and taught me the reality of spirits and so this opened my mind and my world. I also honor all my many Pagan, Craft, and occult friends who initiated, guided, and worked with me in a variety of circles. I honor and am grateful to those who have joined me in running and howling with the wolf spirit. Finally, to all the wild animals, forests, mountains, rivers, oceans, trees, and plants, and all the aware living spirits who reveal the sacred true reality of Nature, to her we say: To you, from You: All things. All things are alive.

CONTENTS

Foreword ix

Preface: The Fabric of the Living World xiii

Acknowledgments xix

Introduction: Me and My Animal Spirits 1

PART I
Discovering Wild Nature

1 Walk on the Wild Side 9
2 Return to Deep Nature 19
3 Sensing Nature 25
4 Instinct, Intuition, and Insight 41
5 Your Primal Spirit 47
6 Communing with Spirit-Kin Animals 53

PART II
Feral Magick Practices

7   Ritual Tools for Feral Magick 65
8   Unleashing Your Animal Self 79
9   Discovering the Genius Loci 91
10 Understanding Spirit-Kin Animals 97
11 Classifying Sacred Animals 107
12 Embracing Your Spirit-Kin Animal 127
13 Deepening Your Spirit-Partner Connection 137
14 Bonding and Trance States 149
15 Shapeshifting 159
16 Intuitive Feral Spellcraft 169
    Conclusion 181

    Bibliography 185

FOREWORD

Denny Sargent's *Feral Magick: Unleash Your Inner Animal Self* is a primal invocation, a howl into the wilderness of the soul, calling forth the lost and forgotten spirits of nature that still stir in our blood. A fascinating and experiential dive into the realm of what the author calls Neo-Animism, *Feral Magick* is a veritable manifesto for rewilding consciousness, an urgent and electrifying reminder that we are not separate from nature, but of it.

Sargent writes with the fervor of one initiated by direct contact and communion with these spirits. He does not merely present dry, historical notes on animism or offer disconnected theories—he takes you by the hand (or rather, by the paw) and leads you deep into the woods to where the spirits of the land, the wind, and the animals speak. His own encounters with the great wolf spirit form the foundation of the work, but this is not merely a personal journey: it is an invitation. To walk this path is to shed the programming of civilization, to discard the chains of domestication, and to stand solidly in accord with the spirits of the natural world.

Feral Magick is structured into two parts. The first, Discovering Wild Nature, is an initiation into seeing the world as it truly is: alive, pulsing, and filled with intelligence. Sargent strips away the illusion of human superiority and guides the reader into an experiential understanding of neo-animism—not as an abstract concept, but as a living, breathing reality. Through practical exercises, meditation, and trance techniques, he teaches how to silence the mind and *listen*—to the rustling leaves, the whispering rivers, and the growl of unseen presences lurking just beyond the veil of ordinary perception.

The second part, Feral Magick Practices, delves into the rites of communion. Here, Sargent shares techniques of shapeshifting—not literal transformation, but a deep energetic and psychic identification with one's spirit-kin. The exercises on trance states, ecstatic movement, and animistic spellcraft are doorways into a raw and untamed consciousness. He speaks of bonding with animal spirits, entering altered states of awareness, and working magick—not from dusty tomes, but from the living pulse of the wild world itself.

What sets *Feral Magick* apart from many books on shamanism and animism is its sense of urgency. This is not a detached academic text—it is a cry, a call to awaken. Sargent does not coddle the reader with soft mysticism; he demands immersion. He speaks of running naked beneath the moon, of throwing off the weight of human constructs, of returning to the deep rhythms of the Earth. There is something dangerous about this book, something that stirs in the gut—it forces you to confront the truth of your own nature. Throughout I was reminded of Austin Osman Spare's concepts of atavistic resurgence, and it's clear that the author has a depth of practical experience in these realms. (Atavistic resurgence refers to the reappearance of behaviors or traits, inherited or otherwise, that have long been absent from a population.)

This book is not for everyone. If you seek a sanitized, domesticated, and academic exploration of animism, you will not find it here. If you are uncomfortable with rawness, if you fear what lurks in the forests of your own mind, this may not be your path. But for those who have felt the call—the restless itch to break free from the suffocating sterility of the illusion of modern life—*Feral Magick* is a map back to something sacred, something vital, and something older than so called modern civilization itself.

Feral Magick is a book that does not simply inform—it transforms. It stirs something ancient within the bones and awakens a primal fire in the very blood of our veins. It reminds us that we were never meant to be tame, that the spirits of the land are still calling, waiting for us to remember. This is a book for the seekers of deep nature, for the wanderers of the twilight places, for those who feel the pull of something wild and ineffable just beyond the edges of perception. Denny Sargent has given us more than a book—he has given us a key. The question is: will you use it?

Awooo!

—Gregory Peters, author of *Yogini Magic: The Sorcery, Enchantment, and Witchcraft of the Divine Feminine* and *New Aeon Tantra: Secrets of Typhonian Magick and Western Tantra*

PREFACE

THE FABRIC OF THE LIVING WORLD

"The world is full of persons, only some of whom are human."
—Graham Harvey, *Animism: Respecting the Living World*

Take a moment to remember a time when a hike in the wilderness entranced you and made you stop in wonder. You breathed deeply, relaxed, and let the beauty and power of nature surround and fill you. Birds sang, trees swayed, you felt incredibly alive. The woods filled your senses and the incessant chattering of your mind fell silent. In that moment, you opened to the beauty, wonder, and joy of simply being immersed in the glory of nature as its energy flowed around and through you. At that moment, your spirit reached out and touched two things: the ethereal world of Animism and the intuitive understanding of the feral magick that manifests in the natural world.

What you experienced was much like the Animist worldview of our Paleolithic ancestors, which is still ongoing today. Animism is a state of consciousness we can enter whenever we choose to remove the barriers in our mind and open ourselves up to that world. This was and can still be done with the conscious use of feral magick—the rites, rituals, and spells of working with the spirits of nature.

This book offers simple ways to enter this transcendent world of primal nature and, in doing, experience spiritual unity. In this way, you learn to work with the many spirits of this world. An Ulchi Siberian shaman I knew and interviewed once taught me that, to form deep relationships with the conscious powers of nature, you must go where the powers of nature are. You can do this by rediscovering and unleashing your own animalistic self so you can communicate with these spirits as equals. Entering this most ancient mystic world is like traveling in a completely alien country with a very different culture.

When I moved to Japan, I was completely lost until I learned the Animist worldview of Japanese culture. It was only then that I could really understand and communicate with others. It wasn't a language issue; it was a very alien worldview to me. I had to accept that everyone in Japan saw the world as filled with spirits and magickal forces. Everyone carried *omamori*, or feral magick charms—for protection, love, success, health, and other aspects of life. All of these were empowered by *kami*, or spirits. Some of these kami were powerful, akin to gods; others were simpler and were more primal spirits—like the spirit of Mount Fuji, to whom many shrines are dedicated.

Japan is also the home of many animal spirits, like Ookami, the ancient and powerful wolf spirit who has many shrines there. This powerful great wolf spirit was the spirit who came and saved me long after I returned from Japan. At first, communication with this wolf spirit was confusing and alien to me. It wasn't until the great wolf spirit showed me techniques and exercises to enter a deep animalistic trance state that our communication became more comprehensible and I moved deeper into the Animist world.

To connect with, communicate with, and bond with animal spirits, you must rediscover and come to terms with you and your own primal animal self so you can communicate with them as equals, much as shamans—just as believers in Animism have been doing for thousands of years.

Animism, New Animism, and Neo-Animism

There are three terms used in this book concerning Animism. Let me clarify.

Animism: According to Graham Harvey, a popular academic and author on the subject of Animism, Animism, which rejected "old animism," emerged with Irving Taylor, an English anthropologist, in the late 1800s. Irving used the modernized term *Animism* more in line with anthropology, leaning into 19th-century cultural evolutionism. In his works on primitive culture and anthropology, he also defined the context of the scientific study of anthropology.

New Animism: Often referenced by Graham Harvey, New Animism emerged with the work of the anthropologist Irving Hallowell in the mid-1900s when he lived with (and began really listening to) the Ojibwe tribe of Canada. The Ojibwe explained that "the world is full of people; some are humans." This changed Hallowell's perceptions; he began to see that, from the Animist point of view, *to be a person does not require human likeness.*

Hallowell began to see from the point of view of tribal people: that animistic spirits are real. Thus, the term "New Animism" became accepted. Graham Harvey uses this term quite a lot in his books.

Neo-Animism: In this book I am using a wholly new term because I feel that it is important to shift our perceptions past the antiquated Animism of the 1700s, and even from New Animism, which is semi-accepted as real. Neo-Animism is the full acceptance that tribal people are right: that all things are indeed alive, and the world is full of nature spirits.

In short, I have crossed the line from academic to believer. My MA is in Ancient History and Intercultural Communications, but I also am a Pagan. I believe that all things are alive. Neo-Animism is the belief that nature spirits are not just real but also are accessible if you open your reality framework and truly *see* Nature, as many of the tribal peoples I have spent time with do.

We Are Animals

The beginning of this path is to accept on every level that we are animals. This takes some deprogramming work, because Western culture has taught us from birth that we are not animals. We are superior, we are told. We have souls, and God gave us dominion over the animals, who are soulless, as well as over all of nature. If we stay within this narrow worldview, we cannot contemplate and experience the spirits of nature. We cannot practice feral magick unless we recognize that we are part of nature—we are animals and spirits, as are all living things. Knowing this opens the door.

The key to success in accomplishing this powerful shift lies in the dynamics of your own primal animal being. Your animal self is very real. It exists within your atavistic or unconscious mind, but it has been denigrated and smothered by civilization. The atavistic mind is centered in your lower cortex, what Carl Sagan called the "dragon mind." This deep animalistic part of you arises during times of stress or situations where instinctual motivation and immediate actions supersede thinking.

We have all been there! We often fall back on instinctive actions that are not driven by higher cognition or thinking. It is our primal bestial self that makes us run out of a burning building or swerve to avoid a collision before our thinking processes have even kicked in. This is the realm of the animal self, which is key to what is called "body memory." This is the deep, dark, reactive place where intuitive and primal feral magick arises—the magick that mambos and witches and shamans rely on when they listen to and work with spirits, cast spells, and perform impromptu rites. Occult books or grimoires are not always necessary in nature's Animist world. Here, the spirits guide.

Feral magick works because our animal selves are rooted in the DNA encoding that is embodied within each of us. We each contain the genetics of *all living things* because all life arose from the first living cell. This is why our human DNA is 98 percent the same as that of a chimpanzee, and 87 percent the same as that of a wolf. This is the reason why we are born with deep intuitive connections with all animals, as well as with the spirits of animals, but we have forgotten this connection. Connecting with animal spirits *as animal beings* is ritually accomplished in many tribal cultures through what is called "atavistic resurgence," the arising of inner animal powers. They do this through feral rites and trance states, just as the ancients did. Amongst many tribal people I have come to know, this is a normal part of their ritual life and a key to their magick.

As children, we intuitively know that we are alive with these animalistic energies. We run wild and free—in and out of feral states of consciousness. Then our parents, schools, and culture reprogram us to fit into the "real world," causing us to forget that this magickal world still exists. The goal of this book is to reawaken the wonder you experienced as a child and help you remember your own wildness.

Once we discover and accept our bonds with animals and with the powers and spirits of nature, we can learn to work with such primal spirits. To accomplish this, we must acknowledge that animal spirits are our brothers and sisters. They are your kin. If we believe we are separate from animals, we lose our ability to communicate with the animal spirits with whom we wish to work.

Shamans tell us that communication is possible only between equals, and there can be no relationships without communication. We can start this transformational process by going into the wilderness and opening our mind and our senses, stilling our mental chatter, and *just being* with everything around us. Just be alive, interconnected, flowing, and present. In silence, we open our senses, we relax, feel the root of all magick—without thinking, we can sidestep our ego and truly perceive how everything is alive and interconnected.

This is the beginning of opening to the Animist worldview—to the primal web of life that is wondrous and ever-changing. When you can accept that nature is full of interwoven energies and spirits that can be seen or even entered—when you are guided by your own feral animal self—then you can acknowledge the reality of personal relationships with these spirits and powers, as many ancient peoples did. This interaction with the vast living web of nature spirits is the basis of practical feral magick.

A loving and conscious relationship with animal spirits was integral to the practices of ancient hunters. The Animistic views of tribal hunters tell us even today to greet the deer as a fellow being, request and honor the deer's sacrifice, then kill it humanely—*if it offers its life to us*—and then eat its flesh with humility and gratitude. Use the whole animal. In the modern world, we are often disconnected from the food we eat and thus disconnected from the spirits of nature that provide it. This blindness further separates us from nature and the animal spirits. This is self-destructive.

Feral magick awakens in us a mostly forgotten point of view in Western culture, one that is now becoming more popular. We need to rediscover and accept the reality of the spirits that inhabit nature and then work with them in order to return to a more natural way of living. The fastest way to do this is to accept the reality of our own animal selves and awaken to our own place in the infinite web of nature. When we become part of the collective Animist world, we can be accepted by the spirits that animate it. This is the heart of feral magick, through which the real intuitive and natural work takes place.

When you open up to the world of Neo-Animism—when you leave behind your ego and assume the primal consciousness of your animal self—the rites, rituals, spells, and other practices in this book will come alive. You will be intuitively guided as the spirits help you. From that point on, your feral magick will become a more creative and impromptu personal dance with the spirits. This is how you unlock the deep powers within nature and within yourself.

May the animal spirits and all the spirits of nature guard you and guide you, and bring you happiness and loving wisdom! Success in your wild work!

Denny Sargent

ACKNOWLEDGMENTS

I would like to acknowledge the help and support of the amazing people who supported and helped me go deeper into the material and experiences of this book. Much thanks to my supportive esoteric human friends whom I work with on multiple levels. I'd especially like to thank my "Starwood Pack," who encouraged *Feral Magick* and had me present crucial parts of this work at Starwood Festival 2024 in the most beautiful, powerful, woodland sacred space where we all called upon the spirits with astounding results and joy. I give honor and love to all the nature spirits and animal spirits of nature, especially the wolf spirit who has always guided me in this. Finally, thanks to my amazing dog Faunus and my werewolf friends: You know who you are and may you never forget that everything is alive.

INTRODUCTION

ME AND MY ANIMAL SPIRITS

I was always a wild child. Even as a toddler I lived in a world where everything was alive and spoke to me in a secret language all the time—until, that is, I was taught by parents and teachers that such things were not real.

Luckily, I have recovered from that indoctrination.

It was a different era, and my parents let me run wild. I was so lucky; I lived in an old house with a huge yard, adjacent to woods and surrounded by a vast wooded and grassy neighborhood. From the beginning of spring on, I ran amok outside all day. I wore shorts and sometimes a shirt; but I almost never wore shoes until I went to school. Tarzan was my role model. I wandered off into this amazing green world, followed by dogs and other critters.

I knew that everything was alive because I saw it. Luminous trees, flowers, and even imaginary friends were always with me, along with other feral neighborhood kids. We ran wild as pirates or explorers until the dinner bells rang. It was a Nirvana of endless trees, flowers, animals, and mysterious hidden places. I spent a lot of time in a huge magnolia tree with massive flowers. That was my "good-energy place," and only a few trees talked to me like that magnolia did. I just assumed that this magickal world was the way things were.

One day while playing with a goofy friend, he became a tiger and began to pace and roar. It was awesome! Instantly, we all joined in and transformed into big dangerous jungle cats, clawing and caterwauling, and arguing about which big wild creature we each were. I vividly remember how real it seemed as we stalked each other.

While running wild, we made friends with all the animals we encountered and were especially fascinated by the woods and wild critters. We made friends with garter snakes, opossums, raccoons, various-colored squirrels, crows, blue jays, mice, shrews, worms, bees, dragonflies, and more. I was perhaps the most feral of our tribe. I was obsessed with holding and playing with garter snakes and sometimes hung them around my neck. This freaked out the other kids, but the snakes and I got along well. One day, for some reason, I created a snake-god idol out of papier-mâché and set it up in an abandoned shed I called the temple. I told my friends that we were now a part of a snake cult and that I was the leader. I have absolutely no idea why I did this or why they followed me! I made them pray to the snake god, but we soon lost interest and wandered off to play another game. To this day, I still love snakes and actually wrote a book about the Naga or snake spirits!

I always loved bees; they never hurt me. But the bees and I both hated wasps. One day, I rescued a half-drowned bumblebee. My parents would have smashed it, but I made a small house of leaves for it and brought flowers to feed it. This went on for days. I chattered with my bee friend and it crawled on my hand and talked back. After a few days, when its wings were dry, it felt better. Mr. Bumblebee crawled on my hand and we visited until it thanked me and flew away. Since then, I have always been very close to bees—especially bumblebees—and have never been stung. (Except by wasps. Grr!)

I also had a special relationship with the lone opossum that lived behind our house. I surreptitiously threw food to it. Then one day, my dad caught my opossum friend near the garbage cans and got out his shotgun! I was horrified, but the opossum was so terrified he simply fell over and played dead. My father picked it up and dropped it in the garbage can. Once he left, I opened the lid and spoke to my friend. I knew it wasn't dead. After a time, the opossum opened its eyes and we smiled at each other. From then on, I left the lid loose on the garbage can so my friend could find food.

When I was around ten, a pair of doves decided to nest in my window frame. By then, my family had become aware that all animals seemed to be my friends—much to their annoyance at times. I kept the curtains in my room closed to give the doves privacy, but once the eggs were laid everyone came to see them. We talked quietly to each other every day and I brought the mama bird worms. In return, she proudly showed me the eggs and, later, the babies when they hatched. We were all very excited—even my brothers and parents. When the dove family moved on, they thanked me, and I wished them all well. All of this seemed normal to me.

At fourteen, I convinced my mom to drop me off on the Appalachian Trail in upstate New York and then pick me up a week later. That's how I met the "deer people." One night, I slept in a field and was awakened just before dawn by a sound. I arose naked from my sleeping bag and there was a large doe standing right next to me! Startled, we both pulled back a bit, but then leaned closer to each other. We began to communicate wordlessly. She acknowledged me as a friendly animal and went back to grazing.

I watched for hours, my mind wide open to this experience. When two small fawns peered curiously from behind the mother doe, she just glanced at me and kept eating without fear. I could have touched them. For hours, they stayed close to me. Then the dad deer with huge antlers showed up with a look of surprise on his face. This vibrant fearless being communed with me and decided I was safe. I was in awe. He came closer and bowed to me, so I bowed to him. In my strange liminal state, this all seemed natural. At sunset, I lay down and the whole deer family settled down and slept very close to me. I was accepted as an animal by these "people" of the forest. I will never forget this experience; it changed my life.

By the time I was fifteen, I was into punk rock and was a more proficient camper. While hiking the high-peaks region of the Adirondacks, going up to Blueberry Lake with a group of friends, I had an astounding encounter with a huge black bear. As I sat quietly, enthralled by the gorgeous landscape before me, I slipped into a trance state and opened up to nature and its animal spirits. Suddenly, there was a scream, and a fellow camper came running toward me from the outhouse. Lumbering behind her was a huge black bear. Rather than being afraid, I was completely enchanted and felt nothing but joy that this massive bear was coming to visit. Stupidly, I felt no fear, just happiness.

As the bear came closer, I realized how gargantuan it was. On all fours it stood higher than six feet and its head was huge. I grinned as it came within inches of me and looked right into my eyes. As I silently greeted it, its huge nose touched my chest. It sniffed me, returned my greeting, and silently "spoke" to me. I was in an ecstatic state, communicating with this beautiful being. Then someone yelled, "*Get out of there, Denny!*" Everyone else was on top of the cabin, of course. So I said goodbye and my friend turned around and lumbered away. My heart was racing a bit, but I felt very blessed by my encounter with this spirit bear. I still do.

I became enamored of otters as a child as well—maybe because I have always been a water animal myself. Once, when I was in the San Juan Islands, I sat meditating on a beach seeking balance, when a huge sea otter waddled out of the water and came right up to me. It leapt up onto a log and sat and stared at me. Suddenly, I found myself in a trance state. I was filled with calm and healing. After a long meditative, silent communion, this spirit otter whistled some otter words to me. It said, "See ya!" Then it waddled back into the water, its work clearly done! I then went wading too, much happier than I had been before the visit of my spirit friend.

But perhaps the most significant encounter I ever had with an animal spirit was with the great wolf spirit. Long ago, after a cataclysmic period in my life in which I literally lost everything, this spirit came to me as I was meditating. This was the first animist encounter I'd had since I was a child. The wolf spirit appeared to me during my regular meditation, but I ignored it. Nonetheless, it kept appearing every night. When I finally got irritated and asked why it was coming to me, it replied: "You called to *me*! You called to me because you are in bad shape. I am here to help you." All of this was true; I was deeply depressed. I had nothing to lose, so I asked him what I should do. He answered: "Go! Go into the wilderness! Unleash your animal self! I will guide you."

And that is what happened. I ripped off my clothes, howled as I released my animal self, and immersed myself in the wilderness. With the guidance of my wolf spirit guru, I emerged renewed and transformed. I have bonded deeply with this spirit for the last six years, and he is still with me and helping me in many ways. I can be found in the woods howling with him when the moon is full. Sometimes we are joined by other feral friends.

Before long, I found myself diving deeply into a more primal magickal world as my wolf mentor opened the gate to Animism—what he called "the wildness." And that descent into wildness is what has prompted me to write this book.

"Write, honor the Spirits!" So growled my mentor, the pushy three-eyed spirit wolf. So honor to him. And honor and love to all the spirits of nature. May they bless you, empower you, and bring you joy.

Awooo!

Denny Sargent
Winter Solstice, 2022

PART I

DISCOVERING WILD NATURE

CHAPTER 1

WALK ON THE WILD SIDE

There's a lot to unpack when it comes to the word "feral." It comes from the Latin *ferus*, meaning "wild," and this nicely describes the magick of pragmatic Animism, the belief that all things are alive and embodied as spirits.

When the word *feral* is used to describe humans or the magick we do, it becomes even more relevant. Some simply define feral as "wild" or "existing in a natural state." A more complete definition describes a feral animal or person as a wild being that was once domesticated, but has reverted to a wild condition following an escape from captivity. If we look at this from the point of view of the growing revulsion many feel towards our current dysfunctional culture and emerging dystopian world, it describes most free-thinking people I know.

In fact, feral magick practitioners have indeed reverted to the wild state after fleeing domestication in order to work with wild magick. Feral magick can be summarized as magick that is unfettered, nature-oriented, free of captivity, and, most of all, wild. In many ways, this describes all Pagans. If this shocks or horrifies you, this kind of magick may not be for you. But my guess is that, if you are reading this book, you saw the title of this book and your wild inner beast grabbed it. How very feral of you! You may be one of us!

The practices described in this book can be defined as "wild magick." They operate on intuitive spiritual principles that acknowledge and work with the spirits of nature, focusing in particular on the spirits of animals. This is the active magickal work we do within an Animist setting or paradigm. It is therefore understood that the magickal feral person identifies as an animal within nature. This is a biological fact that escapes most humans. The key to this magick is to unleash your animal self, your primal spirit being, and join the Animist universe as an equal. I refer to this inner animal, the part of yourself that calls to be released from "domestication," as your animal self. This animal self can be unleashed by entering primal trance states and shapeshifting into the feral being you truly are.

This process does require a lot of letting go—of domestication, of our toxic, stifling, anti-life culture. However, once you have shifted into an unfettered, wild being, the world of nature spirits and their powers is open to you.

Animism teaches that all things—trees, mountains, lakes, and animals—are spirits. But it is the animal spirits that have the most agency. They have evolved over thousands of years to help guide, free, and protect us. Animal spirits have been helping people, especially people who have accepted themselves as being one with animals, for millennia. A good example is the dangerous dire wolf who decided to protect us in our caves rather than eat us. If you have a dog, it evolved from ancient wolves. This bond goes deep. Case in point, consider the wolf spirit who came to me and freed me. What animal spirit will call to you and change your life when you unleash your animal self? Open the gateway for animistic spirits and the animal spirit that is right for you will come.

Animism, and the feral magick that arises from it, is an ancient, yet ever-new, ever-evolving magickal path with no set dogma or rules. It is grounded in an intuitive acceptance of the spirits of the natural world. It leads to you form relationships with all kinds of spirits that call to you and want to help you become a wilder, happier, freer being. It is a pragmatic, open-source process rooted in nature and in direct communion with spirit. It is not dependent on any orders, or holy books, or grimoires. It requires nothing beyond basic civility toward all spirits and acceptance of the fundamental fact that all is alive and interdependent within nature. The goal of its practitioners is to exist in a primal state of consciousness that frees them from the blinders placed on them by their cultural programming.

Breaking Free

We live in an amazing, but toxic, cultural paradigm—one that is nothing like the aware and open Animist world of Paleolithic hunter/gatherers. The simpler, wondrous world that surrounded our ancient forebears was a natural universe that teemed with both abundant life and many dangers. It was filled with spirits who taught them much about life when they were treated honorably as fellow aware beings. Our ancestors saw the world as filled with people, only some of whom were human. In fact, animals, trees, rocks, mountains, rivers, lakes, and plants were alive and conscious, and spoke to those who could hear and see and communicate with them.

Proof of this spiritual worldview covers the walls of ancient caves in the form of images that indicate spells and teachings, some as much as 40,000 years old. Today, we honor those especially sensitive or psychic humans who see these spirits as shamans did in tribal cultures. But in the past, everyone accepted the presence of these spirits and the free-flowing world that was open to them and in constant flux. Animist cultures survive today—in Australia, Africa, South America, and Asia—in which people still believe in the spirits and work with them daily.

Animists see that all beings are born, grow old, and die, and then become spirits that live on as all other spirits that fill the world. The Abrahamic religions radically changed that ancient belief by declaring that those who die are gone forever. Nonetheless, many feel that these departed souls are still with us and can help us and bless us. This belief that the spirits of the departed are still with us is fundamentally animistic. Spirits have always been alive and with us.

In Japan, the Shinto religion, "the way of the spirits," pervades everything. Shinto offers us a modern example of what I call Neo-Animism and pragmatic feral magick. For example, in Japan, cars have spirits, and new cars are ritually purified (*harae*) with a wand adorned with paper streamers called a *haraigushi*. This type of ritual, which I refer to as feral magick, accepts the modern Neo-Animist point of view as a viable and more fundamentally true vision of the world of spirits that we live in: "All things are alive." Many tribal cultures teach that it is the animal spirits, the most potent children of the Earth Mother, who guide us and help us survive. Unfortunately, however, most Western cultures have rejected these teachings and forgotten these crucial natural voices.

I have felt an increasing love for the feral world ever since the wolf spirit broke through my wall of modern Western conditioning and revealed the world of the spirits to me. And this belief in the primeval heart of nature still transforms me. My goal in this book is to help open this door for you. When you break out of your cage and escape domestication, you leap into the Neo-Animist world of authentic wildness and feral magick. And this is when your eyes and heart open to the feral spirits who will guide you into the true reality of freedom and wonder.

For this transformation to occur, however, you must take three important steps: reintegrate with nature, acknowledge your animal self, and connect with animal spirits.

Reintegrating with Nature

All feral magick is empowered by Gaia, Pachamama, the Earth Mother, the most powerful manifestation of nature, the one who gives us everything. There are many gods, goddesses, spirits, and other divine forces with whom we can work, but none is closer to our souls, our DNA, or our very existence than the Earth Mother herself. All that lives on or above or within this planet we call home derives from her. While the sun—and to a lesser extent the moon—empowers, energizes, and regulates the natural world and our bodies, it is the Earth Mother who sustains us, embodies us, and grants us immediate and continual gnosis, if we enter her world. As an Ulchi Siberian shaman once told me: Every footstep upon the earth must be a prayer of gratitude to her.

Unfortunately, this knowledge is something from which most civilized peoples have completely cut themselves off. It has only been amongst the tribal peoples of many countries that I have found this primal, all-powerful magick and ethos still alive. The corrosive effects of organized religion, hypercapitalism, and the delusion of human supremacy are continually destroying the cultures of peoples who live in nature amongst the animal and plant spirits.

To practice feral magick, you must be embodied in nature. You need to identify and embrace a sacred place in nature where you can step away from the civilized world in which you live and step into an environment suffused with wild magick—a sacred green-filled place where you and the Earth Mother can connect—where you can commune with animal and plant spirits.

You can always begin to build this relationship by connecting with the *genius loci*—the conscious energy force that embodies the spirit of a potent place in nature in which you are working (see chapter 9). You can connect with that spirit first.

To do this, get to know your nature, your vital center. What animals live there? Birds? Mammals? Fish? Amphibians? Reptiles? What animals travel through your vital center, but don't live there? Coyotes? Crows? Herons? What insects live here? Butterflies? Ants? Scorpions?

Once you have become familiar with the spirits that inhabit your sacred space, move your awareness of their wild magick outward in an expansive way. Open your perceptions to a higher state of consciousness and connect with the primordial animalistic part of your own being. Remember, we all share DNA with all the animals from which we have evolved. And once you recognize this fact, you can reach out to your own animal self.

Acknowledging Your Animal Self

Take a moment to look in a mirror and say out loud: "I am an animal!" This is a fact, not an opinion. And truly accepting this fact is the first step on the path to feral magick. We have been programmed to believe that we are not animals—that God gave us and only us special, divine souls and that animals are just mindless creatures with no spirits. We have been taught that we have dominion over nature and the animal world, and that we can simply discount them. Yet we are indeed animals. Science has shown that humans and great apes are members of the same zoological family—the hominids. The false belief that we are not animals is the greatest divide between us and the natural world. We cannot work with the forces of nature if we don't accept that we, too, are animals and an integral part of the natural world.

As animals, we each have a primal animal spirit, what I call the animal self. This is the key to our ability to communicate and work with animals and animal spirits as truly free feral beings. Our animal selves connect us to nature and the spirits. They allow us to accept that we are a vital part of the natural world and give us agency to save it or, as we are currently doing, destroy it. This dance between our awakened animistic consciousness and the pragmatic world in which we live is what manifests as the free-flowing magick that embraces the natural world and all the spirits within it. And this wild perspective can help us live more conscious lives and perhaps save our planet.

My experiences with Guatemalan, Oaxacan, and Ulchi Siberian shamans have taught me a lot about ancient animist practices. These shamans use their gifts to work with their sacred animal spirits, performing soul retrieval rites and helping others as they journey through the spirit world. They are able to relate to these spirits because they grew up in a cultural environment that allowed them to see and experience the spirits of the natural world as objectively real. Most encountered many kinds of spirits, even as children. By contrast, those of us who grew up in Western cultures are taught to fear these spirits, as such things are "scary" or "evil," or we are simply taught not to believe in them at all. Thus we need to work at deprogramming ourselves before we can even acknowledge these spirits, much less work with them effectively.

Connecting with the Neo-Animist World

Once you have reintegrated with nature and acknowledged your animal self, you are ready to connect with the Neo-Animistic world. This requires a kind of "shapeshifting" in which you enter into trance states and open yourself to and begin to perceive the spirits of nature that exist all around you (see chapter 15). It will be up to you to reach out to these ubiquitous spirits through your own animal self. Eventually, you will be ready to welcome the specific animal spirit or spirits that are waiting for you.

In the Animist worldview, everything is alive and sentient. There are few rules in this world, but perhaps the most important one is to respect all living things and the spirits that animate them. Accepting and utilizing your animal self allow you to bond with nature spirits through your powers of instinct, intuition, and insight, which arise from the deep unconscious and the animal self (see chapter 4).

Because every situation, and every person, is different, this process is more akin to an intuitive art than analysis. Feral magick is a very personal practice. Much of my own feral work has been guided by the wolf spirit that came to me in my hour of need. But it is important to understand that the natural world is in constant flux and the animal spirits that may respond to your need at any given moment come to you; you don't call them. Your path and your work with the spirits will be unique, personal, and unpredictable. But you can be sure it will be powerful.

Working with animal spirits is a free-flowing, intuitive practice—one without rules that is guided by your animal self and your will. Once you have awakened to their reality, the spirits that come to you will do so because they feel a connection with you. As you explore liminal or trance states in nature, this will make sense to you because you will feel a kinship with the spirits—especially the animal spirits who come to mentor you and bond with you. You will be feral equals and, once these relationships form, your partnership will be open, unfettered, and intuitive.

Animal spirits may relate to you in many ways. They may come as protectors or mentors. They may open your mind to a deeper consciousness. They may heal you, or motivate you, or guide you down the best paths. They may offer crucial information or spiritual links, or make suggestions concerning your animal self and the deep feral powers you have suppressed. They may help you see and work with the energetic weave of your own and every other ecosystem—what is called the *Wyrd*. And, just as they have for thousands of years, they may guide you and assist you in all kinds of magickal work.

Traditionally, shamans call on animal spirits in their powerful work and their healing ceremonies. They reach out to them for protection and guidance when traveling in the spirit world, perhaps to help hunters find elk and other game. Rest assured that the nature spirits with which you connect will teach you and guide you as you navigate the strangely alive and almost-alien world of nature. Some—like the spirits of trees, mountains, rivers, stones, ponds, and waterfalls—may be more shy and less aggressive than animal spirits because they are slower and more rooted in the spirit realm. They tend to offer direct sensations, intuitive feelings, and primal wisdom on deep levels, while animal spirits may be more active and offer ongoing communications and interactions.

It is important to note here that your "favorite animal" may not be the spirit-kin animal that comes to you. You may end up working with a different being entirely. For example, I love gorillas. I collect gorilla images for fun and send contributions to the World Wildlife Fund to protect endangered gorilla populations. But I have never been approached by a gorilla spirit. Liking an animal is different from having an animal spirit come to you in dreams or visions. When this happens, it is an indication that this animal may want to work with you and help you. And this attraction, if you accept it, opens the way for the practice of feral magick.

CHAPTER 2

RETURN TO DEEP NATURE

"I think animism started 100,000 years ago, totemism 50,000–45,000 years ago, and shamanism 30,000–35,000 years ago."
—Damien AtHope

Feral magick is about returning to an ancient, deeper way of being centered in the primordial world of deep nature from which we came. To return to this way of being, we need to reconnect with the spirits and powers of the natural world that have been patiently awaiting our return. Once you have returned to an awareness of deep nature and your integral part in it, you will be able to gain direct experience of the spirits that inhabit that Animist world. When you open to this reality, the spirits of nature will welcome you, bond with you, and help you. This is the heart of feral magick.

To return to the primordial world of deep nature, you must first accept that the spirits and energies that animate nature exist. Only when you become aware of and accept this animistic reality will you be able to experience them. Millions of people around the world believe in and interact with nature spirits. And many work with them often—especially in tribal cultures. Yet our modern cultural constructs blind us to the richness of this world. People simply believe what they are indoctrinated and taught to believe. But with effort and practice, you can broaden your perceptions and unleash your primal animal self, thereby removing the cultural and religious blinders that have restricted your awareness. When you "wake up" to the wild world of Neo-Animism, you find yourself in a world that is filled with many amazing spirits and awesome powers. You become one with myriad beings who together weave the divine flow of life.

Opening Yourself to the Wild

When you wake up to the wild world of Neo-Animism, you will find yourself in a natural world that has always been there, just below your level of awareness. You enter a vibrant biome of living beings that opens your mind, your feelings, and your senses to the spirits and energies of nature. With some practice, you can train your jabbering ego-mind to become still so that your cultural blinders may fall away, and then you can see a world that has been hidden from you or that you were taught to ignore. We all see what we are taught to see. But once you perceive the true world of vibrant, living, and conscious nature, you will likely never go back to seeing the world as the depressing mechanistic place you were forced by your conditioning to accept as reality.

The fact is that the only way you can truly enter this world and work directly with the forces and spirits of nature is to access the deep consciousness embedded within your primal animal self. It is through this that you then can claim kinship with other animal spirits.

The good news is that this is actually easy to do, because you are already, in truth, an animal. Remember how, as a small wild child, you ran around screaming and laughing and full of unconscious physical wildness and joy in the world of nature? You were alive, free, and aware of the amazing magickal world all around you. Everything was amazing, interesting, alive! The world was full of astounding things—crows that talked to you, trees that welcomed you, birds that circled above you, and animals that chittered in overhanging branches and played about you. There were strange forces everywhere and the world was full of opportunities to feel and see new and amazing things! You likely had "imaginary friends" who were quite real to you, special trees you spoke to and sat in. The woods were filled with hidden animals and mysterious energies and so much more.

You were born into a wondrous, ever-shifting realm where everything was alive and spoke to you. That is, until the door to that magickal world was slammed shut by adults who firmly told you what was real and what was not. They discounted your active imagination and slowly smothered your intuitive perceptions. The trees, birds, friends, animals, and fairies of your vibrant childhood world became invisible and nature became a materialistic logical place totally lacking in wonder, rather than a vast living source of joy. You were told it was time to "grow up," to "get serious," to recognize what was real and what was not. Yet most of us remember that wonderland of childhood fondly and miss it in some way.

There is a way back to this halcyon reality of wonder! Your vibrant spiritual self, your inner wild spirit, can still access that imaginative world and the innate joy in nature that you felt there—although perhaps somewhat smothered. In fact, it is easier to break out of the shell of cultural indoctrination than you may think. Part of you has always wanted to.

Think of all the negative lessons you were taught as a child: *Stop acting like an animal! Don't horse around! You eat like a pig!* All wild animals are dangerous and to be feared. Dreams and imaginary beings are not real. Plants and animals don't have feelings or souls. They exist for our pleasure and nourishment. So much fear and negativity instilled. So many doors closed. So many narrow cultural and religious beliefs and lies imposed. And yet, the truth is that the reality that you used to remember as being open and joyous is quite real, although many of us have become blind to it. Nature spirits are alive because *all is alive.* Moreover, these spirits are ready and willing to interact with us.

The key is to reopen the door that was slammed on your childhood beliefs. You have to chip away at the false reality that was imposed on you and unleash your imagination and your childhood memories. Accept that *you are an animal,* a part of nature. Connect with your animal self and spend more time exploring wild nature in a more open state of being. It is time for you to reclaim the joy and wonder you once enjoyed.

Connecting with Wild Spirits

Once you have reclaimed the joy and wonder of wild nature, you can begin to connect with the spirits that animate it, and especially animal spirits. In fact, you may have had an animal spirit or two trying to get your attention ever since you were a child. And maybe that's why you are reading this book! Maybe it is a bear spirit, or a horse spirit, or a crow spirit, or, like me, a wolf spirit. I had to have my whole wall of denial smashed by the wolf spirit after he had been trying to communicate with me for a decade. (This is why he is included in the acknowledgments.)

Once you have opened to the world of deep nature and the idea that it is alive with spirits, it becomes easier to accept that you are a part of that world yourself. You are a feral being. You have an animal self. Working through this transition requires effort, but once you succeed, it follows naturally that you are an animal spirit just like birds and dogs and raccoons and horses and deer. When you connect with your deep, primal animal self, it opens your consciousness to all the nature spirits around you. And this new view of the world allows you to connect with those spirits because you are one yourself.

Like any mental shift, this requires work. And part of that work is opening yourself to the animal spirits that feel right to you. In chapter 11, you'll find worksheets that can help you determine your animal spirit orientation by getting to know the characteristics and history of different animals and the spirits associated with them. As you do so, the animal spirit that is drawn to you may well emerge.

Regular explorations of wild nature are another way to become more familiar with the spirits that reside there. Once you feel a connection to an animal spirit, you may begin to feel a connection to a tree spirit as well. And before you know it, you will become aware that there are a lot of other spirits out there! An Ulchi shaman once told me that it is not uncommon to have several animal spirits working with you. In fact, you may find yourself surrounded by a variety of nature spirits once you open yourself to the wonders of that wild world. So go slowly at first and take one step at a time. Just remember to remain open to the wonder.

Once you have connected with an animal spirit, you must nurture that connection through careful and consistent interaction. Your budding relationship with it will be only as strong as you make it. So be sure to put sincere effort into developing that connection into a deeper, more intimate bond. Think of this evolving interaction as being similar to building a really close friendship—but a spiritual one. Think of the spirit in the same way you would a travel friend or a hiking buddy—someone who can help you and give you advice, but also someone you can have fun with. Your animal spirit may give you wisdom or reveal deep truths to you. It may encourage you to do things you need to do, or even protect you. Just remember to show it respect and respond with gratitude. Relationships are always two-way streets.

When the bond with your animal spirit becomes stronger and more powerful, your magickal work will also become more potent. As you experiment with some of the rites, rituals, and practices in Part II of this book, pay attention to what works for you. Consider which practices expand your consciousness and deepen your connection with the spirit world. Your animal spirit may make recommendations or ask you for things. Or it may suggest ways that you can help yourself or others. The wolf spirit urged me to send money to the Defenders of Wildlife to help protect wolves. And it has saved me from many problems by warning me about certain situations.

This is what spirit friends are for. If the suggestions of your spirit partner feel intuitively right, *pay attention*. My wolf mentor has shared a lot of ideas, questions, and practices with me that have enhanced my own instincts and intuition, and enriched my own magickal practice. In fact, some of the most powerful experiences I have had have come through the quiet mentoring of this spirit.

May you enjoy and find enrichment in the adventures and wonders revealed in the realm of nature and in this book. May "The Other" open for you and may the kind animal spirits who seek and call to you bless, empower, and help you. May you open yourself once again to the astounding miracle and wonder of the world you once lived in as a child and so rediscover the manifold joyful Nature Spirits as you evolve and awaken to the magickal animal you are within nature.

CHAPTER 3

SENSING NATURE

"All we have in our brain is an interpretation."
—Dr. Rudy Behnia

The culture in which we are embedded tells us that, on every level, this is a materialistic world. Plants are not sentient. Animals do not have souls. We are the only intelligent beings. We have been told by several faiths that God gave us dominion over everything. But that is patently untrue. The amazing unfolding world of nature and the animals and plants and rivers and more that abound here existed long before primitive man appeared and will be here long after we are gone as well—unless we can avoid self-destruction and once again accept and work with nature and all the spirits that abide here.

Animals have unique intelligences, as do plants and fungi. Science has revealed that trees help each other share nutrients and that fungi create vast underground networks that interact with other plants and support the environment. Complex ecosystems have been studied for ages, yet recent scientific analysis shows that they are so vastly complex and interconnected that we cannot completely understand how they work. All living things work together intuitively to survive and prosper. When circumstances change, they adapt. It is only the ravages of modern humans that threaten to destroy them.

Ironically, however, it is the seemingly conscious web of life found in complex natural ecosystems that offers us an objective way to talk about nature spirits. The consciousness characteristic of the complex interrelationships found in natural ecosystems remains beyond scientific understanding. And yet ancient (and current) Animist tribal cultures understand it well. They know instinctively that the explanation lies in the flow and interactions of nature spirits that are active and vital and alive in their own way. They were and are fully aware of how these spirits interacted because they are raised as a part of this miraculous and astounding reality. For thousands of years, they have acknowledged this flow of energies and worked with it as part of the world in which we live.

By simply observing nature and the forces and animals within it, Animist cultures learned how to use those interrelationships to work with and live a harmonious life. They experience the physical world as working in tandem with the mysterious spirits of nature and the spiritual way in which all living things are woven together. The ways in which the spirits of nature and nature itself interact and support each other still teach us how to live, what to eat, how to hunt, how to honor animals within nature, and how to work with the animal spirits connected with them. In short, they lived within the flow of nature and the spirits that inhabited their world. And this worldview persists today.

In this chapter, we'll explore several ways you can learn these same lessons by engaging your five senses to help you enter and understand the world of nature spirits as you interact with a wild natural location. In a sense, this amounts to what I call "sensory reprogramming."

Sensory reprogramming encourages a shift in consciousness that can bring you into a direct experience with wild nature and its animating spirits, and open you to a new way of perceiving this world. This in turn will prepare you to interact with the animal spirits that will support you in your practice of feral magick. Our brains take in information and then shape it to fit our preconceived notions. Our modern upbringing has programmed us to differentiate between what is real and what is not. I remember how shocked members of a tribal culture in the mountains of Thailand were when they realized I could not see the spirits living in certain trees or large stones, or in their sacred river. We simply see what we have been programmed to see.

But if you want to work with nature spirits, you have to *see* them. You have to get out from under your cultural programming and perceive them as part of a Neo-Animist reality. And the best way to do this is to let go of your mental expectations and open your mind to the energies of the natural world. You have to approach new experiences in nature with all your primal senses activated and your mind free of preconceived notions.

Choose a relaxing forest or an isolated trail in nature for this work. The wilder, the better. The fewer humans, the better. Wear comfortable clothes and bring along some fresh water. You can also bring seeds, nuts, or berries as offerings to the spirits you will encounter.

The sensory reprogramming described here may not work the first time you try it. If that is the case for you, simply do it again. With time and effort, you will find a way to open your primal being and natural consciousness so that you can connect with the world of nature spirits.

Opening Your Primal Senses

What is the world we live in? Everyone's experiences are different. Some say that all our perceptions are holograms, created by what we expect to see and believe. Some trust their senses, but most people are also thinking of other things and not really focusing completely. Yet shamans, meditators, and those who are serious about magick have been opening up the "doors of perception" for eons within wilderness settings, shutting down their ego and really perceiving everything. Many experience phenomena for which they have no explanation, because such things are so new that they cannot comprehend "strange things" or really "see" them. Our senses and our brain are mostly taking in information already programmed in our database and matching it with what we believe we are seeing.

The truth is we see what we expect to see, what we *know*. This is why our brain cannot be counted upon to correlate completely new information about our environment. So, what is our path to really understanding the Neo-Animistic world? The goal is to "step sideways," so to speak—to shift to a new a state of consciousness in which you can actually perceive the unusual and be able to accept things like nature spirits. Stop trying to simply *believe* in spirits, and concentrate rather on perceiving them. "Seeing" is accepting. To enter the realm of nature spirits, open your mind in a new way. The most obvious way to do this is to enter the wild natural world, the wilderness, with a silent mind, in a calm and relaxed light trance state. Any wild, unspoiled forested hiking trail or wilderness park largely devoid of people will do. Relax and open your mind and inner spirit to new experiences. While used by the ancients, hallucinogens or entheogens are not necessary for this gentle experience. Just take a relaxed walk in the woods with your senses fully engaged, your mind totally still, and your consciousness wide open. Focus on what you sense around you, and you will soon begin to feel the presence of nature spirits.

Approach the wilderness in a relaxed but focused mood, without thinking about anything. No cell phone, no talking, no deep thinking, no distractions. The more silent your mind, the better. Walk slowly and focus intently on seeing everything around you with a dreamlike open mind. Notice the small details. The challenge is to experience pure nature directly, without engaging your mind. Just settle into a calm, relaxed state as you wander and experience the wildness. Settle into a light trance state, one without thought.

See nature as if you have never seen it before. When the chattering of your mind fades, focus on breathing deeply and feel completely calm. Let the stress of your life evaporate in the fresh, clean air that fills you with each breath. Simply be. As your heartbeat slows and your deep breathing calms you, focus on the beauty in everything you see around you. With each deep breath, let yourself sink into a meditative state of liminal consciousness. Enjoy the lightness and the luminous quality of every tree and flower. Stop thinking completely. Let the power and energy of nature fill you.

Once you are fully immersed in this meditative state, begin to gently open the perceptive gateways to the Neo-Animist world by focusing on each of your four remaining senses in turn. In this way, you will "step sideways" into the vital world of spirit.

Call of the Wild

Like our sense of sight, our sense of hearing is subjective. What we hear is filtered by our brains and by our expectations and conditioning. We believe that we really hear words or sounds accurately, but we can decode them only in the context of what our brains have already stored. This is partly due to our neurological structures and our linguistic centers. But it has a lot to do with our cultural conditioning as well. When we hear the sound we identify as a hawk, we can understand that sound only if we already know what a hawk is and what it sounds like. And because of how our brains work, we miss most of the meaning and importance of the infinitely varied sounds of nature.

But you can learn how to focus your primal being on the many sounds of nature and truly hear and comprehend their deeper meaning, even if you can't recognize what those sounds are. Just as you "sidestepped" into a new state of consciousness by accepting what you assumed you saw, you can open your mind to truly listen to the myriad sounds of nature and open yourself up to their meaning by shifting and really opening your sense of hearing.

It's really not that hard to do. Stop "recognizing" sounds; be open to all possibilities. As you wander in nature, just let your mind settle into a deep liminal state, breathing deeply and slowly, and strolling at a pace that lets you truly absorb the beauty you see everywhere without intellectualizing. As you enter a light trance state, pause and focus all your consciousness on hearing nothing but the natural sounds around you. Close your eyes and continue to breathe slowly and deeply as you let the musical sounds of the woods wash over you and embrace you. At first, the infinite variety of sounds will merge into a single subtle wave. After a time, however, you will begin to isolate some of the sounds; some will become clearer, more intense. As you walk, focus in on the many sounds you hear as birds speak with each other or sing or call to their mates. As you begin to isolate individual sounds, consider how the threads of those songs are connected. Let your mind open to a dreamlike understanding of the sounds and the meaning of each song. Suddenly, each becomes meaningful.

Now shift your listening focus. Listen to the whisper of the wind as it breathes gently through the trees. Hear the rustling music of the leaves and the creaking of the branches. Close your eyes. What do you sense? What images and thoughts come to you? What are the trees saying to each other? What are they saying to you?

As you shift your listening focus again, you realize that there are a number of quiet, subtle sounds deep in the woods, many of which you had not heard before—rustling, humming, slithering. And suddenly you know that the many-layered, vital life of nature is whispering to you and that what you are hearing is the infinite variety of nature spirits weaving the vibrant web of life that constitutes the world of wild nature. Let the many small sounds of that wild world fill your open consciousness, crowding out all thought—wind, trees, birds, scampering critters, a chattering creek, rustling grasses. A whole symphony of wild sounds, rising to a crescendo that threatens to overwhelm you.

As this esoteric symphony fills your senses, let your light trance state take you farther into the liminal world of the nature spirits—a world in which these intricate sounds suddenly take on meaning, resolving into a hidden language in which you begin to discern messages and meanings that dangle just barely out of reach. Through this intricate web of vibrating sound, the spirits of nature speak to you, communicating the truths

you need to know in order to open your mind to the authentic reality of their world. As your senses shift and adjust to this new reality, you become more intensely aware of the wild nature around you—the whispering of the tree spirits as they commune with the wind, the splashing of the water spirits as they refresh themselves in the creek.

Listen to all these voices as they call to you, even if you cannot fully understand them. Be open to their hidden meanings. You will soon realize that they have different rhythms, different pitches, and different tones. They flow and shift and create complex harmonies. And when you let your primal inner self, your animal self, become aware of these rhythms and harmonies and the messages they carry, you hear the call of the vibrant web of life that is nature. The croaking of frogs, the chittering of squirrels, the calling of crows, and the rustling of deer are all part of the vast interconnected dance and vital flow of wild nature. The spirits of trees, the spirits of animals, the spirits of rocks and creeks and the wind are all offering up a hidden melody of life. Let your intuition and subconscious insights drink in that song. Hold the mysterious thoughts, feelings, and images that it evokes deep within you, silently thanking the spirits for this amazing symphony.

Once you have shifted into this deep perception, this new way of truly *hearing* the sounds of wild nature, ask the spirits to help you isolate a simple sound or rhythm that will help you return to this state of consciousness whenever you need to reach out to them. Then listen for something special, something that stands out from all the complex harmonies you hear—a simple repeated rhythm, a sequence of soft humming sounds, a lyrical whistling. Repeat the sound you hear three times, then wait for a response. If it comes, you will know that you are beginning to commune with the nature spirits.

Whatever simple sounds you hear and use as mentioned, remember them. Such sounds are keys that will grant you entry into the wild world of nature spirits. For millennia, tribal cultures have used specific tones or whistles to facilitate their work with spirits. The spirits cannot "speak," as such, but they can communicate in their own way. You will be amazed as you travel deeper into wild nature and the liminal world of spirits just how much they want to work with you and connect with you, even though many in the modern world appear to have forgotten them. When you open to the sights and sounds of nature, you become one with the spirits that inhabit that world. And they, in turn, will acknowledge you and seek to communicate with you.

Primal Scents

Our most primal sense may be the sense of smell. And this most animalistic sense can help you enter into and explore the wonders of wild nature. When you focus on awakening your primal sense of smell, you reactivate many animal instincts that are an integral part of your animal self.

Our once-crucial animal senses and instincts have been largely suppressed by our modern Western culture. There are only a few scents that get our attention these days—perhaps something like a gas leak. Whereas animals and Animistic cultures focus more on immediate sensory reactions, today we spend more time thinking than we do on actually experiencing what surrounds us in our environment. Our attention is most often engaged by the hectic demands of daily life rather than by the needs of nature. Our inner animal, our primal feral selves, may be awakened briefly—for instance, when we smell a fire or sense other dangers. But in these cases, our autonomic nervous system and lower cortex take over and prompt physical reactions.

These moments reflect our pure animal instincts. Unfortunately, however, we have lost touch with the instincts that allow us to sense or deeply perceive other states of being. Although many shamans in tribal cultures have retained the ability to slip in and out of "normal reality" and commune with spirits, most of us have lost our innate sense of the spirit world because we have been brainwashed most of our lives to believe that mundane, "normal" reality is the *only* reality.

It is interesting that, in our Western culture, many believe in angels and ghosts, but not in nature spirits. This tells us a lot about our cultural and religious programming, and how our perceptions have been conditioned by them. Our modern "civilized" brains have disconnected from our primal selves and from our animalistic survival instincts, to the point that we no longer see ourselves as part of wild nature at all. In a sense, we have become disconnected from the authentic world of nature and now focus entirely on the intellectual, abstract, and computer-driven world of everyday life. No wonder so many of us are depressed, unhappy, and detached from a natural life.

When you focus intently on your sense of smell, you reconnect with the biome and your most primal animalistic being, your animal self. Try losing yourself once again in nature. Relax near a tree or a bush and take several deep breaths, then open your awareness to the varied scents of the location you are in. As you walk slowly, let these earthy smells fill you to the exclusion of all your other sensory input. As you do so, quiet your mind and deepen your meditative trance and slide deeper into the liminal world of primal nature. Immerse yourself in a wave of natural fragrances. Breathing deeply, release all thoughts of the mundane world, and embrace this richly scented world. Smell the flowers, moss, and even the leaves. Pay attention to the differences in their scents. Smell fresh dirt and stones with real focus. Inhale the sharp aroma of pine needles, and the musky odor of different leaves. Drink in the fresh smell of a creek, a spring, or a lake. Explore everything with your nose. As you marvel at the beauty and uniqueness of each scent, let your instincts take over. Let your mind and body and feelings react. Don't think. Just focus on your feelings and your insights. Be open to experiences that arise in you.

What do you *feel* with each scent? What insight does each bring? Which experiences excite you? Which calm you? Which repel you? Which ones arouse you in some way? Accept and deeply sense those feelings. Experience the reactions of your body and your instincts without analyzing them. As you explore these sensory reactions, begin to pay attention to more subtle smells—the aroma of various kinds of moisture in the air as you walk, the distinctive bouquet of the sap from different trees, and even the difference between the odor of a new oak tree and an older one. The scents of pebbles and wild flowers and salmonberries may all change your feelings and your moods, and may at times fill your primal self with joy. Each fragrance can evoke a number of visceral reactions from your unconscious mind that may manifest as visions, memories, or emotions. All of these experiences will reawaken within you a deep connection with nature. You will soon realize what a delightful experience it can be to smell your way through the wilderness!

All of nature responds to and the entire natural world is triggered by the language of this vast flowing together of scents within your brain and this complex wild ecosystem. The various scents of the wild world support a vast web of interaction and interweaving of plants, rocks, soils, insects, microbes, and animals. We have lost our instinctive knowledge of this vast sensual network that connects all living things—except perhaps when we go to a supermarket and feel and smell the produce!

As you learn to embrace all the scents around you, open yourself to everything, all that you have experienced. Breathe deeply as the power of wild nature engulfs you and all your senses. You may smell something new and strange—maybe something floral. You may feel the caress of the wind or even see some odd ethereal movements out of the corner of your eye. Because the truth is that, as you fully open your senses intently on the living world of nature, more than you ever have before, you open your consciousness to the Neo-Animist world of the spirits that inhabit it. In fact, you have taken yet another step into the living core of deep nature.

Reach Out and Touch a Nature Spirit

In order awaken to the Neo-Animist world as a living part of your own animal self, you must physically connect with it. This calls for consciously touching, handling, or caressing the living "beings" that inhabit that world.

As with the senses of sight, hearing, and smell, you can accomplish this by "sidestepping" into a new state of consciousness in which you can literally reach out to nature and experience it through your sense of touch. Try rubbing your hands together while shifting your focus to your sense of touch. Relax and breathe deeply, then refocus your being on your primal sense of touch. Touch your hair, your arms, and your legs. Focus on the marvel of your tangible physical self and, as you do so, awaken to your inner self—your animal self, the animal you are. Concentrate on the concrete reality of the physical world as you shut down all your senses except that of touch. Then rub your hands together until they feel nice and warm and become more sensitive. Hold them before you and focus on this sensation and the warmth and tingling you feel.

As you settle into a light trance state, stand before a tree that calls to you and close your eyes. Reach out and touch the tree's trunk. Let your hands wander slowly across its bark, then carefully reach up and gently touch a sprig of leaves or needles. Feel the different textures and the coolness of the branch. Let the feeling flow through your nervous system. Then find different trees that call to you and touch them slowly, noting the differences and the variety of sensations. Marvel at the infinite variety of the natural world.

Now try the same thing with moss and lichen, and finally with several different stones or rocks. Pay attention to how very different they all feel and observe your visceral reaction to each sensation. How does each touch make you feel? Pause between each tactile experience and open yourself to your deeper *instinctive* reactions. Which trees feel protective or healing? Which plants change your moods or thoughts? Which stones calm you? Which ones energize you? Does anything you touch repel you?

After considering these reactions, breathe deeply, place both your hands on the ground, and open yourself to the Earth Mother. How does your primal being react? Hold on to those primal feelings and reactions. Then touch another tree, then another rock, then some more moss. Process these experiences in a deeper primal reactive manner based in your contact with the Earth Mother. Intuitively feel and embrace your inner self with each touch. Let your experiences resonate with the power and whisper of each being you touch.

Try taking off your shoes and socks and letting your feet do what your hands have been doing. These different sensations will open up new feelings and experiences. Close your eyes and accept the energy of the Earth Mother as it flows into your body. Find some soft loam or moss or grass to walk on. Dig your toes in and focus on the feelings, the energy, the whispers, and the visions you receive. As these tactile experiences fill you, let them open you to the magickal world of wild nature. Give your reactions voice through a simple repetitive humming or other primal sound. Don't force it; just let these things happen naturally. Sense how the spirits all about you react to your touch. Do you sense water spirits reaching out to you? Do the trees and grasses whisper messages just for you? Does the birdsong you hear seem to be telling you something? As you explore these primal experiences—these intuitive communications, these visions, these messages—be aware of how they change your state of being.

Do this as a walking meditation many times, in many different forests, and your deepening perceptions will unfold and open levels of awareness you never experienced before. When you are done with each sensory exploration, sit and meditate on the sensations you experienced. Consider the interactions you had—consciously or unconsciously—with the physical living energies of nature and the spirits they embody. Note this process in your journal as your experiences grow and your understanding of the spirits deepens.

A Taste of Nature

We have already seen how awakening your senses of sight, hearing, smell, and touch can open you up to an awareness that everything in nature is alive with energies and that those energies are embodied by spirits. Now let's look at how refocusing your sense of taste can take this shift one step farther.

Taste is perhaps the most profound and accessible way to connect with nature spirits. We focus a lot of our energy and attention in life on our sense of taste. Every meal, every snack, every sweet treat, every cup of coffee, and every glass of wine fill our brains with a mix of sensations, memories, and feelings. Enjoying the taste of wild berries or savoring the flavor of chives is a joy. But so is experiencing the sweetness of a light breeze in the woods or tasting the salty tang of a breeze at the beach. We enjoy the taste of fresh, pure water and the tang of pine needles, and even treasure the taste of a kiss. In fact, our sense of taste offers us a primal, neurological experience that is emotional and spiritual, offering connections and reactions. Moreover, our sense of smell and our sense of taste are closely connected, and one often elicits instinctive reactions from the other. We smell the fragrance of roses; but we taste the scent as well.

Refocusing your sense of taste to support an authentic experience of wild nature can be a little tricky because you wouldn't usually just go out and chew on a tree or nibble on a rock. This requires a little more subtle approach, one grounded in an even deeper liminal state than you experienced while addressing the other four senses. To achieve this state, go back to your favorite spot in wild nature and begin a quiet stroll. Relax and breathe deeply, with your mouth slightly open. With each breath in, still your mind and allow your senses to focus on the taste of the forest. Take your time. As you move closer to a pine tree, then a maple or a raspberry bush, inhale and notice the subtle differences in the taste of the oxygen and sap each tree is emitting. This will take a little time and some intense focus, but the differences will soon become clearer.

As you wander, relax and enter an even deeper liminal state of calm, while sharpening your taste perceptions and silencing your mind. Once you are comfortable with your in-breathing and "nature tasting," pause at a particularly potent place that seems to offer more intense "inhaled flavor" and close your eyes. Focus only on what you are experiencing and inhale slowly, drinking in the rich savor of the whole forest. Always bring water with you on your explorations. Drink some of it and marvel at how rich it tastes. When you come to a pine tree, or maybe a maple tree, nibble on the tip of a single needle or maple leaf and focus intently on the complex flavors. Continue as you like but make sure that anything you sample is safe to eat. As you nibble, close your eyes, and silently open yourself to the spirit of the tree with love. Breathe deeply. Be open to what your mind's eye perceives. Then open your eyes and bow to the tree in silent thanks. Try this with a blackberry, then try it with a blade of grass or another safe wild berry, like a salmonberry. Let the complex experiences of each taste-trance fill you and speak to you. Let each taste excite aspects of your primal animal self and elicit feelings of each living spirit embodied in each berry and leaf.

The tastes of nature may be subtle at first. But as you focus more intently, each will become more comprehensible. You will find that your expanding focus awakens subtle differences depending on whether you are "tasting" a breeze or the moisture rising from a creek or the smell of flowers. Each experience will elicit increasingly powerful feelings and reactions, and this in turn puts you in touch with the vital, active spirits around you in nature.

Once your mind and perceptions are awakened to the nature spirits, locate a large tree that you can feel and even "taste"—a tree that emanates energy. Breathe deeply and raise your arms, then extend your own energy toward the tree. Let your eyes go out of focus a bit and open yourself to the spirit of the tree. Use your intuition here. Perhaps just breathe deeply or hum a tune that fills your consciousness at this moment. Silently open your primal self as you reach out to the tree that calls to you. Center yourself; breathe deeply and close your eyes as you open yourself to the spirit of the tree. You may sense its spirit, or see it, or connect with its presence in another way. Gently commune with the tree and let it connect with you for a time. Taste a small part of the tree. Leave your mind open to feelings, visions, colors, or symbols that come forward as a result of the encounter.

While in communion with the tree spirit, begin to expand your sensation of taste using your other senses. Gently open your senses of hearing and sight and smell and touch as you continue to taste the "breath" of this mighty tree. Let all your senses embrace the joy of this spirit. After a time, open your senses to the spirits of all the trees around you. You may be shocked by what you feel, sense, and see as you suddenly become aware of all the nature spirits that surround you. You may sense or feel or perhaps even see glimmers of these presences, or you may feel in your mind that they are present and curious or happy or shy as you have awakened them to your presence. Once they know you are "seeing" and "sensing" them, they will be as interested in you as you now are in them.

When you open your mind and your senses to the world of wild nature and to the spirits who inhabit this amazing living wilderness, you will find that you can see and hear and feel and taste and touch a more authentic world than the one you have been taught to accept as real—a world of swirling energy and dancing light and life. Take a moment to open your arms wide, breathe deeply, maybe hum, or sing, or gently howl, as you open and embrace this Otherworld. Once you have experienced that world, be sure to show it respect and love. Let the energy of the nature spirits fill you and feel their power. Open your inner spirit, filling yourself with all the power of nature and your body in love and light.

As you leave the wilderness, don't speak for a time. Just hum or make sounds that come to you naturally. Try to keep your mind still. If you must think, meditate on nature and the infinite web of energies and spirits that supports this vast spiritual ecosystem. You have awoken to the authentic spirit world of plants, rivers, trees, stones, lakes, oceans, birds, and animals. Through your senses, the portals of your living self, and through your own primal spirit, you will experience the truth—that all things are alive. All things are conscious in their own unique way.

Welcome to the real world. Welcome to the Other.

CHAPTER 4

INSTINCT, INTUITION, AND INSIGHT

Once you have shifted your perceptions by reprogramming your senses, you are ready to experience nature spirits directly. The key to accomplishing this is to accept what you have experienced in wild nature and use it to connect your primal feral being to the natural world and the spirits that inhabit it. Open up your newly focused senses and call into service your newly shifted perceptions. Rely on the innate skills of your animal self. Let your senses lead you. Listen. Feel. Then wait for the energies and spirits of nature to reach out to you.

This involves utilizing your instinct, your intuition, and your insight. Your instinct allows you to act without thinking. Your intuition gives you access to immediate knowledge. Your insight connects you to your primal animal self. Each of these resources operates in a different way to give you direct experience of deep nature.

Instinct—Reacting without Thinking

Instinct reveals itself most often in your physical reactions. Have you ever walked into a place and immediately gotten goosebumps? Or felt a tingling that tells you something is there when nothing can be seen? Have you ever walked through the woods and suddenly had your senses alert you that something is near? In many of our current cultures, we are taught to ignore these subliminal messages. But in many countries and communities around the world, these feelings are considered crucial elements of an awareness, especially of the unseen world. I once woke up in the middle of the night knowing something was wrong and ran into my young son's room without thinking. I found him stuck between the wall and his bed. I hadn't heard anything and reacted before I was even fully awake. Most parents have had this kind of instinctual experience.

When I was living in New York, instinct saved me many times, warning me that a questionable thug was nearby or to avoid a particular alley. On the other hand, instinct once gave me a gentle nudge to walk down a wooded path in Central Park to see a beautiful heron. I often get a physical "gut feeling" that draws me instinctively to some area in nature or away from a "bad place." I sometimes avoid certain areas because I *just know* that is the thing to do.

Your primal animal instincts come to the fore when in nature. They have been wired into you for millions of years. Unfortunately, in our modern world, instinct is often discounted or mocked. But I am here to encourage you to acknowledge it! Hone your instincts. Become open to them and trust them. They are deep and real and part of your essential makeup. When you get a gut feeling about something, that feeling comes from your primal animal self. You are being made aware of what is happening around you and given a chance to allow your primal animal self to assert itself.

As we saw in chapter 3, a good way to learn to "see" the spirits of nature is to learn to open your primal self and sense them. Engage your senses when in nature and be open to the input these experiences and interactions with spirits give you. When your instinct points to a tree that just *feels right,* be open to it and feel its spirit. Sense it. As you walk past several boulders, use your instinct to feel which one is "awake" and has a spirit that is willing to connect with you. Accept these interactions and let the spirits inform your work. Revel in the experience. Remember the feelings or images that come and note them in your journal later. Noting down your experiences in a journal helps you easily recall important thoughts later.

When relying on your instincts as you reach out to a spirit, project a calm interest. The spirit may project a positive feeling, or it may not wish to interact with you. If you instinctively feel no connection, that spirit may simply be asleep. Use your instincts to determine the state of interplay if there is interaction. This may seem somewhat abstract, but in practice I think you will see that it is quite real. Sharpening your instincts will help you tune in to nature spirits and accept their reality. Some people practice working with trees, stones, rivers, plants, and other natural beings because they can be easier to contact than spirit-kin animals. By learning to sense and connect with these spirits instinctively, you can prepare yourself to reach out to animal spirits that may be interested in you.

Intuition—Immediate Knowledge

Intuition is another way in which your animal self helps you sense and relate to spirits. Through your intuition, you can gain deep knowledge of how spirits feel toward you. Unlike the visceral, immediate reactions prompted by instinct, intuition involves opening your inner mind and feeling and thus having an immediate sense of something real. We've all experienced this many times, often without recognizing it. Think of times when you knew without thinking that something was wrong—such as a pet being injured—and found out later that, in fact, something was wrong. Or maybe you felt that it was about to snow at an unlikely time and then, just like that, it started snowing. This is intuitive knowing, connected with your unconscious mind. I remember once suddenly strongly feeling as if I should call a friend who turned out to be very ill. This is how intuition works. It prompts a kind of immediate knowing that occurs without thought or logic.

Imagine you are wandering in nature, open to the spirits around you, strolling about looking at trees, rocks, bushes, and creeks. You take a moment to pause at a tree and, without thinking, you sense that there is a spirit present there and that it is awake. If you are relaxed and not "thinking" much, your intuition can offer you immediate knowledge that there is an awakened spirit near you. Without thinking, feel and intuit your way to connect with the spirit. Close your eyes and "see" its energy. Then mentally reach out to it. If your intuition is open and clear, you will have an amazing experience.

When this happens, focus on the spirit and be aware that it has an individual energy signature. You may feel an intuitive little "ping" that lets you know that, yes, this spirit is here and it feels unique. After experiencing such intuitive successes, these liminal intuitive feelings will become clearer and you will begin to accept them as part of you. This can help prepare you for working with all kinds of spirits.

Animal spirits are not as simple as the spirits of trees or plants or rocks. They are more complex and are often drawn to certain places to which they are connected. Sometimes they are more ephemeral and flightier than other spirits, but are more actively interested in humans. That's why I recommend sharpening your intuition by using it to interact with simpler nature spirits before reaching out to animal spirits.

Insight—Deeper Knowing

Insight is a form of primitive, unconscious "knowing." It is a gut reaction that also draws on deep-mind cognition to arrive at a moment of clarity—although you may not be aware of why some truth or idea suddenly arises in your mind. Insight is what prompts those "Aha!" moments that we've all experienced—moments of realization that arise from the unconscious mind into a powerful "knowing" that is deep within a part of our primal animal mind. When confronted by a problem that needs solving or a puzzling situation, we often step back and let the answer arise as an insight, often when we are not consciously focused on it.

As you explore wild nature and begin connecting and relating with spirits, be sure to pause and simply open your mind without thinking. Then wander until you are pulled or gently nudged toward a specific tree, or rock, or plant spirit that is important to you. This is a moment of insight. You simply *just know* that is a spirit to whom you are drawn, or one who is drawn in you. In fact, there are times when insight can be even more powerful than intuition or instinct. Think of a time when you met someone you just *knew* would be a friend from your very first meeting. That's insight at work. When you are attracted to a particular spirit through your insight, it can be a sign of that spirit's interest in you, rather than you being interested in the spirit. Remember, some spirits may want to reach out to you, and not the other way around.

Often it is important to heed your insights—for instance, when working with a genius loci that has a deep-rooted connection to a place. The genius loci of a wilderness area has more power than many other local nature spirits and may be harder to find. You can wander about looking for it using your instinct and your intuition, but your insight may be much more effective. When you use your insight, you rely not only on feeling but also on deep inner knowing. Opening your mind in meditation and emptying your thoughts help manifest insights. Your instinct and intuition may alert you to many nature spirits, but it is your insight that will help you know which one is the most powerful and conscious. Whether it is a huge mossy rock or a massive tree, you will simply know that its presence is far more intense than that of the other spirits.

When you encounter a deep-rooted spirit like this, honor it by holding up your hands with your palms facing out. This gesture carries friendly vibes and feelings. When your insight leads you to a powerful genius loci, take time to sit with it and work with it. Think of it as a mentor and a helper. Sing or hum. Make offerings of water or seeds or nuts or berries. Open your mind to its wisdom, or just spend time with it. And remember where this spirit dwells so you can connect with it for more serious spirit work in the future.

CHAPTER 5

YOUR PRIMAL SPIRIT

The most important spirit in your world is—well, you! Most religions and spiritual belief systems acknowledge that every human being has a soul or spirit. To me, this is just like trees and animals and all other forms of nature. We are all alive, we are all unique, and we are spiritual beings. We each have a primal spirit that came into the material world with us and will depart with us, perhaps to carry on in some manner. Our primal spirit is the core light that shines from the center of our being, and of course it plays a crucial role in the work we do with other spirits. Moreover, we are not the only ones who have primal spirits. In a Neo-Animist world, everything is alive and all beings have and embody primal spirits.

Are our primal spirits eternal? Who can say? Buddhists believe in reincarnation; others believe in heaven. Shinto priests who believe in both human and nature spirits see life as a river that ends when we pass on, like water passing over a waterfall. And after the waterfall? Who knows? They have no clear answers, except a belief that those with strong spirits may become akin to conscious unfettered nature spirits who may continue their existence in the vibrant world of wild nature. I, for one, know that my primal spirit is real. It radiates a special energy and consciousness that are centered in my heart. It expands and contracts according to love and will. It seems to contract when I am down or angry or being self-centered—glowing and outgoing when I am open and caring.

Like all spirits in the Neo-Animist world, we have agency. And it is from this agency that the power of feral magick derives. That is why it is important always to honor and care for your primal spirit, your inner self, which is the source of power for all your magickal and spiritual work. Your primal spirit is the most important tool you have for working and connecting with spirits. It centers and protects you, and is the fulcrum on which your work with nature spirits is balanced.

It is important to understand the crucial role that your primal spirit plays in your work with spirits, because not all nature spirits are warm and fuzzy. Some are benevolent. But some can be quite difficult. And it is your conscious primal spirit—working through your instincts, your intuition, and your insight—that can help you recognize and deal with both types. *Focusing and activating your primal spirit is simple.* If you feel in any way uncomfortable, just calmly place your hands over your heart and illuminate the light of your primal spirit. When you can "see" and feel the intense light in your core filling your hands, slowly open your arms and allow the brilliant glow of your spirit to shine out around you and before you.

Dealing with Problematic Spirits

Like all living beings, not all spirits are loving and open. Some are problematic; some are asleep or shy. And some are downright difficult. I feel that unhappy nature spirits—found mostly in urban environments or depleted parks or damaged forests—have simply not been treated well. But even in vibrant and healthy natural areas, you may encounter spirits who are not always pleasant. In my experience, however, even these spirits are almost never malicious if you know how to treat them.

Think of times when you met an unfriendly or threatening dog and carefully gave it space. If you encounter an unfriendly nature spirit—whether it is a glowering tree spirit, or an irritated animal spirit, or the disgruntled spirit of a polluted river—your best course is just to follow your instincts. If some dark spirit is projecting a negative feeling, or seems unhappy, or is uninterested in communicating with you, just let it go. Don't react. Don't show fear. Just calmly back off with your palms up and send out a calm neutral vibe. Offer a simple mental "pardon me" and move on. No need to feel, express, or allow fear into your body or mind; such negative spirits will move on if you do.

Your primal spirit can be useful at times like these because it can give you immediate insights that arise from your unconscious mind, perhaps as visions or even dreams. These insights are crystallizations of important truths that materialize suddenly and without much thought at all. Practice calling on these insights as you interact with trees, plants, rivers, and other natural beings. As you become more confident, you can move on to animal spirits. Spend time in nature just opening your senses and being ready to receive nonverbal communication from all the various spirits you find there.

And keep in mind that you can and should utilize your primal spirit (and your general energetic field) when dealing with any kind of nature or animal spirit that is difficult or problematic. This sort of situation is rare, but is worth addressing here. If your instincts, your intuition, or your insight indicate that a newly encountered spirit may be unhappy, angry, negative, or in any way problematic, then it is likely a spirit with whom you do not want to interact. Your best course of action is to disengage gently and move on.

If you feel in any way uncomfortable, again, just calmly place your hands over your heart and illuminate the light of your primal spirit until you can "see" and feel the intense light filling your hands, then slowly open your arms and allow the brilliant glow of your primal spirit to shine out around you and before you. Then calmly and silently will that spirit to move on. If you like, you can vibrate "Ah Ya." Ignore any negative feelings. Instead, just radiate peace and love, and wait until that pesky negative spirit fades away. Then pull the light of your primal spirit back by bringing your hands together. See the light flowing back into your heart, then cover your heart center with your hands to seal your primal spirit back into your core, letting its light and energy fill and protect you.

Verifying Benevolent Spirits

As you begin to expand your work with nature spirits to more complex animal spirits, it becomes increasingly important to be able to verify which spirits are benevolent and which are not. Even if you have already had contact with an animal spirit that is drawn to you, you still need to vet it to determine if it is an appropriate spirit with which to work and possibly bond.

If an animal spirit comes to you in visions or dreams, or through subtle odd experiences, always verify if it is a spirit you want to deal with before getting any closer. Just because a spirit approaches you doesn't mean that you have to accept that connection. Nature spirits have agency. But remember—so do you!

For example, if a crow spirit is drawn to you, do the following: Go outside and sit in silence. Close your eyes and open yourself to the spirit that has approached you. Breathe deeply and slide into a liminal space or a light trance state, then wait until the spirit reaches out to you. Place your hands on your chest and open your primal spirit so that its light shines brightly. But, in this case, leave one hand over your heart.

When the spirit approaches, relax and close your eyes—either partially or completely—so that you feel it as much as see it. Sit and be open to it and meditate in silence with it. Let it communicate with you in whatever way it wishes. Be kind, but maintain your internal silence. Keep one hand over your heart and feel or see the light of your spirit glowing. If it is a nice interaction, and you want to have a connection with this being, all is good. Open both hands as a sign you approve. When done, sprinkle some seeds, nuts, or berries as a kind gesture of thanks. Bow and honor this crow spirit in your mind and heart with humming or even a friendly "Caw!" Offer to meet again and go on your way.

However, if it is not an animal spirit that seems right for you, or if things get weird, or the spirit refuses to depart, simply remove the hand from your heart. Hold up both hands palm out and intently unleash brilliant light from your primal spirit as you will the spirit to *go*. Don't emanate anger or irritation; instead remain calmly focused on your primal spirit. Silently wish the spirit the best with firm kindness and clap your hands three times. Then bring the light of your primal spirit back into your heart and body, clap three more times, and simply leave.

CHAPTER 6

COMMUNING WITH SPIRIT-KIN ANIMALS

"Communication is only possible between equals."
—Robert Anton Wilson, *Prometheus Rising*

In a sense, Part I of this book has provided a sort of spiritual training program in which you have learned how to step outside your civilized box and communicate with an entirely different world. You developed new sensory experiences and enhanced your powers of instinct, intuition, and insight. You cultivated a gentle understanding and awareness of the world of wild nature and learned how breathing deeply and sliding into a liminal state can help you connect with it. You discovered the importance of acknowledging your animal self and have seen how shining the light of your primal spirit can help you manage interactions with all kinds of spirits. And you have also learned how important it is to record all your spirit and magickal experiences in a journal so that you can review them and build on them as you move more deeply into the Neo-Animist world. In other words, you've already done a lot to prepare yourself for the more complex animal spirits that we will discuss in Part II.

Now that you have discovered the world of wild nature and learned how to navigate it, it's time to turn our attention to those complex animal spirits. Before we move on to the specific practices in Part II, however, I want to speak more generally about what it means to interact with animal spirits and how some of the techniques you have already learned can help you succeed in your work. Knowing how to develop and expand your ability to interact with (or avoid) animal spirits and how to call on your powers of instinct, intuition, and insight will be of invaluable help as you begin to reach out to these more complex, more autonomous, beings. And perhaps the most important lesson for you to learn as you start down this path is to understand that animal spirits usually *come to you*!

As you become more open to the "Other" or Neo-Animistic world of spirits, so too will animal spirits become more aware of your work and open to you. They then will often try to get your attention if they find you interesting as you've become more and more able to perceive them. As a new animal spirit taps on your metaphorical window, be open and also ready to decide if the animal spirit which comes to you is the right spirit for you to work with and, if so, how you will proceed. It is likely that you may already have had a sense or feeling—or perhaps even an actual encounter—with an animal spirit. In fact, the techniques we discussed in previous chapters were expressly intended to build the skills you need to deal with nature spirits in general so that you can apply those skills to interactions with more complex animal spirits. And these skills will become especially important when working with your own personal spirit-kin animal.

Finding Your Personal Spirit-Kin Animal

We have entered the realm of the nature spirits, some of which are animal forms or spirit-kin animals. Be aware that such powerful spirits may be attracted to specific humans, maybe you, but they are often not connected with "a favorite animal" you may dote on. Once you have opened to the Otherworld of the spirits, it is possible that you may be approached by a spirit-kin animal, maybe in your dreams, in your yard, or in visions. However, if a spirit-kin animal comes to you and you feel or experience this spirit (and you'll know!), it is important that you be open to connecting with it. Meditate on the spirit-kin animal that comes to you as often as you can, and always have your journal handy so that you can record the experience. It is always best to begin your meditation by opening up your primal spirit and then connecting with your potential spirit-kin animal in mind. This begins to build a bond and opens communication. Opening up your animal self within a meditative framework also opens you to a simple trance and the liminal space of the spirit world. When you acknowledge yourself as the human animal you are, it opens you to communication with your spirit-kin animal. It also calms all the nature spirits and lets them know that you are a positive loving ally who desires a positive interaction with them.

It is important to remember that your favorite animal is not necessarily your personal spirit-kin animal. Spirit-kin animals come to you; you don't generally choose them. I have bonded with the wolf spirit; yet if asked, I would have said that my favorite animals are otters and gorillas. The same may be true for you.

The first step in identifying your personal spirit-kin animal is to acknowledge when such a spirit comes to you. You will learn to recognize the gentle nudging or subliminal "hum" that generally accompanies this kind of contact. If this happens at an inconvenient time or you are approached by a spirit-kin animal you did not expect, you can simply ask it to come at another time. Or you can just accept the experience without questioning. If you choose to accept the experience, remember to open the light of your primal spirit before initiating contact. When you are ready, just exist in connection with this spirit in whatever way you like. And be sure to be open to whatever messages or feelings it shares.

Here are a few things to remember as you communicate with spirit-kin animals:

- ✦ Always honor that spirit-kin animal.

- Always project a sphere of light from your primal spirit that surrounds you both.

- Be receptive; listen and be open to the unusual and sometimes difficult-to-understand communications you may receive.

- Remember that feelings and empathy encourage understanding.

- If a relationship is consistent, accept that the experience you are having is valid and real.

- Shared ideas and positive attitudes are crucial to cultivating your interaction.

- Assume that you are interacting with a very primal being. Show respect and listen, and observe what this being is communicating.

- Be hospitable and emotionally accepting; think of it as a meeting with an important or illuminated person.

When the interaction is over, give a simple offering that is appropriate. I recommend seeds, nuts, or berries because they are all safe for physical animals as well. Of course, a spirit won't eat the food, but the essence will be absorbed, as will the caring the food embodies.

And, of course, always write down everything you experience in your journal.

Getting to Know Your Spirit-Kin Animal

Once a specific spirit-kin animal has come to you and you are both happy with the interaction, it's time to learn more about it. As the relationship between you grows, certain things will become apparent. The mental image you have of the animal when you are in liminal space should become clearer and develop into a consistent visualization.

As time goes on, it should become easier and easier to open to your spirit-kin animal through opening your primal spirit and entering a liminal trance state (see chapter 14). You should become more comfortable building a spirit-to-spirit interaction. And finally, the bond between you and the spirit should grow as you tend it with care and even love. If these things don't happen, meditate on this.

Be sure that you don't treat your relationship with your spirit-kin animal in the same way you would treat a relationship with a living animal. Spirit-kin animals are complex spiritual beings that are unlike living animals or humans. Like venerated ancient spirits or animal deities like Ganesh, they need to be understood as transcendent animalistic spirits, often ancient.

Here are a few key questions you can ask as you begin communing with your spirit-kin animal friend:

- Why are you choosing to work with me?
- What can I do for you?
- How can I better communicate with you?
- How can we strengthen our bond?
- What do I need to learn from you?

Here are a few things to remember as you reach out:

- Keep your questions (whether telepathic or spoken) very short and to the point.
- Be very clear; assume you are dealing with a being from another world. (You are!)
- Such spirits understand basic, primal, clear, simple communication best, whether they be telepathic, spoken, or visualized. Don't use idioms, slang, or complex thoughts or sentences.
- Avoid complicated questions; don't ask for things or advice a spirit cannot understand or relate to.

And never forget: This is not about you and your desires or needs! You're in a partnership with an autonomous spirit animal with its own ideas and plans—one that is working with you, not for you.

As your relationship expands, deepens, and evolves, it will become easier for you to have silent, internal, deep, and often-mind-to-mind communications with the spirit-kin animal that has chosen you. As you become closer, some of these communications may happen in unexpected places—like when you are at work, or when you are with family, or when you are out with friends. Some may be spontaneous. Some may just be off-putting or weird because, again, these beings are not human, nor do they always act in ways that are logical from our point of view. Often, they are unexpected or just unusual for you. That's the fun of it!

Of course, it is always best to communicate with such beings within nature, where the spirit-kin animal is most comfortable. It is a being of pure, primal nature, after all. The best option is the deep woods or nature, but a park, your yard, or your garden can all be great places to work with your spirit-kin animal. Any green natural space full of living things is also a great choice. Try to dedicate a special sacred space where you can meet and commune—with your spirit-kin animal or other spirits you seek—so consider creating a specific place, or shrine, or altar that becomes more familiar over time. (We'll talk more about this in Part II.) As your spirit-kin animal begins to accept you, you too will feel this connection growing. Responding with positive emotional energy can be crucial to building a strong interaction.

As your bond grows stronger, your spirit-kin animal partner may start to communicate in ways that may seem new, odd, or surprising. Unusual events may happen, sometimes suddenly or as if by chance. Small gifts may appear; you may hear odd sounds or tones. Who can say? These occurrences are clearly gifts from your spirit-kin animal—and they can sometimes be quite funny or meaningful as your animal spirit friend plays with you. You'll see. Have fun.

Divine Associations

It is now generally accepted by anthropologists that what I call Neo-Animism was, in fact, the origin of all religions. Some argue that Animism existed from the most ancient human cultures and is the earliest form of spiritual belief, likely originating hundreds of thousands of years ago. Damien AtHope estimates that Animism originated as far back as 100,000 years ago, and totemism developed from it approximately 50,000 years later. Shamanism, he claims, followed approximately 15,000 years after that.

One theory claims that the belief and interaction of humans and natural spirits evolved over many millennia as the perceived nature and animal spirits became visualized and honored as anthropomorphic gods and goddesses. We recognize today such primal deities in ancient and modern religions around the world. Indeed, many cultures today still worship and work with both primal nature spirits and spirit-kin animals but many others have come to see these spirits as gods and goddesses that have taken on human or partly human form.

The animals listed on the next page were once honored by prehistoric humans as spirits that had agency and power. And these perceptions of primal spirituality developed into human deities that were connected to spiritual animal forms (see chapter 11). They were first honored and worshipped for their direct connections with natural elements, and shamanic cultures relied on interactions with these forces to control and give meaning to their environment. Over millennia, these direct forms of worship shifted into the more ritualistic worship of images, like the cave paintings of hybrid animal-human deities found in many locations. These hybrid forms eventually became wholly human in later cultures. For example, the Greek and Roman god Apollo appeared in ancient form as a wolf, while the Hindu god Shiva was depicted as a forest god with the horns of a bull. Even today, many gods and goddesses who are honored in human form are often connected with an animal "helper," like Shiva's divine white bull.

Here are just some of the survivals of animal spirits found in religions around the world today:

- Bears—The Greek goddess Callista took the form of a bear at will. Raijin is a Japanese god of lightning who appears in bear form.

- Crows/Ravens—The Morrigan and other Celtic goddesses often appeared as ravens.

- Deer—The Celtic horned god Cernunnos, god of the forest, was said to appear as a luminous deer. The Norse deer god Eikthyrnir is said to stand upon Valhalla. Elen of the Ways was honored as a primordial British reindeer goddess.

- Lions/Lionesses—The Egyptian goddess Sekhmet, goddess of power, healing, and war, was shown as a lioness. The Roman god Aion was a lion-headed deity who embodied the cycles of the year.

- Snakes—The Vodou goddess (Lwa) Mama Wata is depicted as a spirit or goddess carrying a large snake. Manassa is the Hindu goddess of serpents (nagas).

- Whales—The Hawaiian whale god Kanaloa is still honored as a powerful spirit of the ocean. The whale kami Sama Bakekujira is said to be a frightening Japanese god. La Baleine (the whale) is a Vodou Lwa invoked for protection, prosperity, and fertility.

- Wolves—Lupa, the wolf who found, nursed, and sheltered the twins Romulus and Remus, was later venerated as a deity in Rome and celebrated at the Lupercalia festival. Apollo was often depicted as a wolf, and he and his mother, Leto, often take the form of wolves.

This brief list shows how the feral spark of primal spirit-kin animals has glowed within the veneration of many gods and goddesses over eons. These associations will become important in chapter 11, where we will explore animal spirit orientation.

PART II

FERAL MAGICK PRACTICES

CHAPTER 7

RITUAL TOOLS FOR FERAL MAGICK

There have been many amazing artifacts discovered in prehistoric archaeological digs, some of which were most likely used in animist ceremonies. These items were apparently seen as being "alive" and were used to connect with spiritual beings in the animistic world. A growing number of archeologists are beginning to study how native Americans, such as the Hopi, created and transformed such tools and artifacts into "alive" objects such as vessels and tools that were living items used in spiritual and other workings. They have coined the term "object agency" to describe the power of such sacred items, many of which are still venerated today.

Ancient Pueblo were also artisans such as potters and created pieces of sacred items that were considered to be alive and have agency—meaning that they had the ability to act on their own—for use in animist ceremonies. These items and tools were not just material "things." Their creation and use were rooted in the Animist beliefs that spirit-embodied sacred items were very helpful in many ways, like for healing or spiritual protection. When these objects were used in ritual work, they became "helpers" and even partners in animist rituals and in protective or other magickal workings.

These animist practices were well known in ancient times and many myths refer to "living" objects that held magickal powers. Certain swords were said to be "alive," much like King Arthur's Excalibur, which was said to have a life and will of its own. Many sacred items such as *shabti* or clay protecting spirit figurines were buried with the deceased in ancient Egyptian tombs. Their animistic powers helped protect the deceased in the Otherworld. Some actually had eyes carved or painted on them to indicate their power and agency. While traveling in Australia, I saw 30,000-year-old sacred glyphs that Aboriginal tribes claimed were alive and capable of empowering magick and offering protection. I also saw numerous sacred carvings and paintings, and tools for working with ancient primal animal forms that were said to have been "manifested" from the Aboriginal dreamtime.

In the ancient world, almost all important and consciously manifested items were likely to be seen as alive and filled with magick and agency. For example, ancient musical instruments were often described as living spirits that had their own ritual power. A vulture-bone flute thought to be 40,000 years old was found in a European cave amid fragments of other mammoth-ivory flutes that were likely used in ceremonies and burial rituals. In fact, in many cultures, the sound of a flute was thought to project powerful magickal forces for seduction and love, birth and death, and protection. And this belief in the animistic power of music and musical instruments survives in works like Mozart's *The Magic Flute*.

Potent mystical animistic-enhanced jewels, swords, and various types of vessels have been venerated in Japan for thousands of years and are still honored there today. Japanese shrines are filled with animistic items that are believed to be alive and imbued with spirits. Sacred trees are said to move; torii gateways are said to grant entry into the spirit world; haunted statues are said to be possessed by spirits. The presence of these spirits is often indicated by a *shimenawa*, a woven rice-chaff rope strung with paper streamers, as a sign that a spirit lives there and should be honored. In fact, all tools used in Shinto rites to banish negative energy are seen as spirit-filled and having agency.

In this chapter, we'll look at a number of tools that have traditionally been used in Animist magick and that have proven very useful for practical feral magick work as well. Many of these are still being used by shamans and other indigenous ritualists around the world. I recommend that you acquire a toolkit of these sacred implements so you have them ready to use in the practices and rites that follow. Of course, tools that you create yourself are always the most potent. But you can find them or buy them as well.

Your Neo-Animist Ritual Toolkit

As you build your feral magick toolkit, be sure to bless and cleanse all tools of any negative energy before using them. I do this with pure water mixed with pure salt, but any living water works as well. You can also wave tools carefully through a spiritually blessed flame or smoke. This is a potent and ancient process that many choose to use. Or you can anoint your tools with any pure oil that feels right to you. Just use what calls to you.

When you create your sacred tools with focus, intent, and will, and bless and cleanse them with love, you empower them and imbue them with life. You can also enhance their potency by vibrating sacred sounds, or sleeping with them, or "feeding" them. I recommend that you keep your sacred ritual items wrapped in a clean, natural cloth to keep them pure. As the spirits begin to work with you, let them guide you on how to bless, cleanse, charge, and store the tools you use to connect with them.

Here is a list of some of the tools traditionally used in feral magick.

- **Spirit tablet:** This is a flat stone of any kind that you can use as an altar when working. Try to find a thin one so it is easier to carry. Or you can buy one. I use a thin one-foot-square piece of flat shale that I bought at a home improvement store. But natural stone slabs are easy to find as well.

- **Natural vessels:** These can be shells you have found, small stone bowls, gourds, woven grass baskets, or ceramic dishes. They should be made of natural materials and it is best if they are made by you or created for you. When I travel abroad, I look for these kinds of items in tribal cultures and among spiritual peoples. I have gotten them from artisans in Cambodia, Japan, Australia, Indonesia, China, and Guatemala. You'll need a vessel to hold pure water and one to hold spirit offerings like seeds, nuts, or berries. Make sure these are safe for birds and other wildlife.

- **Natural cloth or blanket:** You will use this to lie or sit on while doing ritual work. You will also need smaller cloths for wrapping sacred items and tools when they are not in use. These are traditionally white, but you can also use red or black. Green is nice as well! It is up to you. Be guided by what the spirits indicate.

- **Medium-size satchel or cloth bag:** You will use this to carry your ritual tools and items. It is best if this is made from natural or hand-woven cloth. But whatever you do, don't use animal skin.

- **Natural animal items:** These will act as links to the spirit-kin animal that is bonding with you. What you use will depend, of course, upon the spirit-kin animal you choose. Some examples include crow feathers, shed snake skins, shed bear fur, coyote bones found in the wild, and similar items. You can also use amulets or talismans that have been specifically fashioned from animal items or from natural wood to venerate your spirit-kin animal.

- **Natural plants:** You will use these in your rituals to honor and connect with the spirits. They should all be collected in nature and may include herbs, pods, pine cones, acorns, dried flowers, and other natural items like leaves, sap, grasses, twigs or branches, or bushes. Let your spirit-kin animal guide you. You can use these dried or burn them, or to make tinctures or teas for magickal protection or healing. Again, let your spirit-kin animal guide you.

And of course, remember to have your journal handy whenever you do magickal work. It will help you remember, analyze, and learn from your experiences as you work with nature spirits of all kinds.

Divine Vibrations

The universe runs on vibrations, and so do our spirits. Our words, our magickal rituals, and our very cells vibrate. In fact, everything in the cosmos and in our world vibrates. You enter liminal spaces and deep nature through shifts in vibration. All animistic practices work with the help of modulated vibrations, as any shaman will tell you. And this how we know that all things are alive.

This may seem like a simplistic way of looking at things, but science bears this out. All things manifesting in the universe are vibrating. Shifts in vibrations alter molecules and atoms and quarks and tachyons. The universe is full of constant change and constant motion. Constant energy shifts are part of the mystical, all-embracing, vibrating, humming reality of the natural world. And you are a part of that world.

Thus, it makes perfect sense that, from prehistory to the present, spiritual practices have involved tones, sound, and vibration. Before our distant ancestors had spoken language or developed complex linguistic skills, they made sounds that had meaning for them and for those around them, likely imitating the sounds of animals. We know this from the tools and simple musical instruments that were apparently used in animist rituals. Remember the prehistoric flutes described above.

Even today, shamans, those who practice meditation and chant, and magick workers use sound to open gateways, call spirits, banish negative energies, heal the sick, and create sacred space. Tones, rhythms, sequences, and vibrations are all powerful tools for accessing and manipulating the world of magick, and they have been used in this way from the earliest times. And this is still true for us as we work with nature spirits in general and spirit-kin animals in particular. Sounds and vibrations can manifest as sacred intent, as focus, as will, as love, as intensity, and as healing. They help to open us to a way of seeing and understanding that allows us to work directly with the spirits.

When inducing trance states, we use the same sacred vibrational tools today that the ancients used to work with and communicate with the spirits. Some of these include rattles, drums, bells, rhythm sticks, hand clapping, whistles, and flutes. And of course, the human voice is a potent tonal "tool" that can reach out to the spirits through humming, chanting, vibrating, singing, or animal cries. In fact, in states of deep trance, we experience various and unique effects when using different vibrational tools to work with different spirits. Different vibrational strategies elicit visionary images that can open the vibrant world of nature to us and may prompt an amazing variety of visions—reality shifting, perceptions fragmenting, waves flowing, colors pulsing, images warping, and even liminal flashes of lights and movements.

Here are just some of the vibrational tools I recommend you have in your magickal toolkit.

- **Rattles:** These can be large or small, and are best when made from natural substances—woven fibers, wood, ceramic, etc.
- **Drums:** These are often small and handheld. They can be two-sided or one-handed, like the den den daiko or damaru.
- **Singing bowls:** These can be made of glass, ceramic, or metal, and the sounds they make will be vastly different depending on what they are made of. They are often struck or vibrated using a wooden wand. Use what feels right for your work and, as always, let the spirits guide you.
- **Bells:** Sets of seven metal bells work best, but you can also use tika bells, handheld bells, ceramic bells, or glass bells.
- **Rhythm sticks:** These are most often made of wood, sometimes bamboo. They should be made of a natural substance and are often created from specific tree branches depending on the spirit you are seeking to contact. They can be decorated in any way you like. Use your imagination and let your intuition guide you.

Here are some ways you can use your own body to generate sounds when working with the spirits:

- **Humming:** Sequences with varied pitches and tones work best. When you use the right sequences, the spirits will often "echo" it in odd ways.

- **Whistling:** Simple sequences of alternating high and low tones work best. They create "waves" in the spirit world and can put you in direct empathic communication with your animal partner.

- **Singing:** You can sing either with or without words. If you sing in sync with a spirit-kin animal or echo its "song," the sound may vibrate with that spirit, causing it to respond in kind. All vocalizations can be songs.

- **Clapping or stomping:** Clapping your hands or stomping your feet are both very primal rhythmic actions that seem to echo in the world of deep nature. Clapping three times with a strong intent empowers and cleanses in animist rituals.

And of course, the cry or "voice" of your spirit-kin animal is the most primal and oldest method of communication in animal spirit work. When you use the sounds your spirit-kin animal uses, it helps to forge a relationship with that animal. Of course, the "voice" you use will depend on the spirit-kin animal you are approaching—growling, cawing, howling, hissing, or many other sounds that echo through the natural world. Take the time to master as many as you can.

PRACTICE

Creating a Spirit Shrine

As you prepare to enter the active world of feral magick, a good first step is to set up a small shrine where your world and the world of spirits can connect. The stone tablet altar is crucial. Such a shrine area is your personal and private place where you can interact with the spirits you call to and which approach you. This sacred space, big or small, will become a kind of home for nature spirits as well as the spirit-kin animals you may work with. It doesn't need to be a large stone tablet or an elaborate shrine, just a simple place where this world and the spirit world can intersect.

The most important item you will need, as mentioned, is a flat stone that can serve as a kind of altar. It is nice if you find such a stone in the wild, as natural stones become imbued with the power and consciousness of the wilderness. However, buying a stone altar is fine, too. Choose one that feels right. Remember, in the Neo-Animist world, all things are awake and alive with nature spirits. And this includes stones.

Decide on the location that you feel is the best spiritual place for you and your spirit-kin animal or other spirits to meet and commune on a regular basis. Traditionally, these shrines face north or east, but that is not necessary. Once you have chosen a place, clean it thoroughly with a little salt water and a clean cloth. Place the stone tablet on a simple, natural cloth—white is best—then open your animal self (see chapter 8) and invite your spirit partner to join you. When you feel its presence, place a few of your tools on or around the tablet, including your water and a small bowl of seeds, nuts, or berries. Then close your eyes, breathe deeply, and center yourself.

When you are ready to commune with the nature spirit or spirit-kin animal, place your hands on your chest and "see" and feel the intense light of your primal spirit there. Open your arms and expand the light into a sphere of light that surrounds you. Begin a simple humming pattern, then pick up a rattle or small drum and set a steady beat as you descend into your primal consciousness along with your animal spirit.

You can place other items on the tablet that honor the spirit as well. Consider adding plants, because the closer you are to nature, the better—even in your living room. I am lucky enough to be able to work directly with the wolf spirit at a stone tablet outside in my yard under massive trees and many plants. But, as always, it is best to let the spirits guide you.

To empower your shrine, visualize that you are standing at the crossroads between this world and the spirit world as you continue your humming and rhythmic pattern. As you enter a light trance state, your animal and nature spirit partner will guide you as, together, you open to the spirit world (see chapter 14). Allow the power to calm you. Then stop the humming and rattling, and deeply commune with your spirit partner in the silence. Listen and be open to its thoughts and suggestions.

It is important to spiritually cleanse your shrine on a regular basis in a way that feels right to you. Burn some appropriate banishing herbs, keep the area neat, or sprinkle a solution of pure water and salt about. Keep it clean. Again, rely on the spirits for guidance. Then bless the area and the shrine using your rattle, whistle, or drum. You can also hum or vibrate words and sounds that feel right. There is no one right way to do this. The spirits will indicate what will help you connect more easily. The wolf spirit guided me to gather sap from a pine tree and some cedar bark and rosemary to burn and cleanse the area of my shrine.

Once you have finished setting up your shrine, you may move it, but know that spirits, like people, can get disoriented! However, you may at times wish to take your stone tablet and other items with you into a forest or to the beach to work with spirits. When you have set up the shrine, take a walk in nature with your spirit-kin animal partner and gather any leaves or herbs it indicates. When you return to your shrine, lay these items on the spirit tablet, then place both hands on it and, with your eyes closed, touch your forehead to it. Call silently to the nature spirit or your spirit-kin animal. Open your primal spirit. Enter a trance and when your spirit-kin animal partner manifests, silently honor it and offer this shrine as a gateway between the spirit world and the mundane world. Cry out three times in your spirit's call. (For example, a wolf spirit's call may be a howl.) Then honor the Earth Mother with a long "*Maaaaaaaaa!*" as you open your consciousness into the earth for a time.

Sit up and be open to the Other. Be open to the spirits. Hum as it comes to you. If the spirit-kin animal is happy, you will know it. Sit and open to all the spirits.

After a time, when the quiet work is done, stand and clap three times, then bow and use your arms to gather in all the light and pull it back into your heart center. Release your animal self and move on with your day. Keep in mind that, when going into the wild to work your magick, you will bring many of the tools and items from your shrine with you. Just be sure to return them to your home when you leave the woods. Maybe keep them on an "inside" altar, a place with honor where they will be safe.

PRACTICE

Blessing Your Magickal Tools

This simple rite can be done for a number of purposes. It can bless and empower your tools and your shrine, but it can also be used regularly to forge an intense connection with your animal spirit. You can do this practice at your shrine if you choose.

Over the next week or so, sit before your stone spirit tablet in silence, and project a sphere of light from your heart center as previously described. Expand that sphere into a larger circle of light around you. Then silently call to your animal spirit with a powerful, intuitive rhythmic humming. Close your eyes slightly and let your focus blur. Quiet your mind, breathe deeply, and enter a liminal space, remaining open to the presence of your animal spirit. If all is well, the spirit will make this clear and establish a connection. If you feel uncertain, commune with the spirit to see what it needs.

Wear simple, clean clothing for this rite—white, black, red, or the color that feels right to you. Your animal spirit may indicate a clear preference. Practice calling the spirit with its appropriate cry—a caw, a howl, or a roar. Bring along some pure water from a living river, stream, pond, or lake. You can also collect rainwater.

For this practice, you will need:

- ✦ A powerful stone or talisman that resonates with your spirit-kin animal. This can be anything that is natural and that feels right. If you are not sure, ask your spirit-kin animal to guide you.

- An all-natural rattle, drum and/or rhythm sticks, or bells. Make sure they are tools that you have used only for previous nature-spirit work.
- Some dried herbs, leaves, or other natural items that have been sitting on your spirit tablet. These can be crushed and placed in a natural bowl.
- Matches (avoid lighters, if possible).
- A natural vessel with seeds, nuts, or berries, or whatever the spirit you're working with might prefer.
- A newly cut flower, leaf, or other green plant that is still alive.

Place all items on the tablet in a way that feels right to you, with the talisman indicated by the spirit in the center. Arrange the tools around the tablet in whatever way feels right to you.

Sit before the stone spirit tablet and breathe deeply as before, inhaling and exhaling to a count of seven. As you do so, place your hands on your heart and open your brilliant primal spirit. See light streaming from your heart and surrounding the shrine in a sphere of light as you open your arms. When you are ready, slow your breathing until it is natural and partially close your eyes. Place your hands together over your heart center and open your animal self. See your reality shift as you open to the spirit world.

Enter a trance state and begin to hum any simple rhythm that comes to you as you silently invite a spirit or your spirit-kin animal to connect with you with love and will. When the spirit joins you, listen to what it says and change your humming pattern as it tells you to. Then take up the rattle or rhythm tool and, as you continue to hum, begin a simple rhythm. Take your time; there is no hurry! As things become clearer and more energized, begin rocking and let the rhythm and humming connect with your movements. You will sense a clear shift in your reality, and your connection with the animal spirit will grow stronger as the energy and information flow.

Once you are in this zone, put down the rhythm tool and take up the pure water, while continuing to hum. Dip a finger into the water and bless the tablet by sprinkling the water all around while vibrating "Haaaa" over and over, making this sound part of your humming song. Your humming pattern may shift as the spirit indicates.

Light the dried greenery in the vessel and wave the smoke around the tablet and tools three times, alternating your humming with the "Ahaaa" sound. Wave the smoke over the spirit talisman and over all the other items, vibrating a long "Ahaaaaa" sound. Then make the appropriate animal cry three times. As you do so, "see" the spirit imbue the spirit tablet, your tools, and the talisman with its power and presence.

Bow before the tablet and take up the rattle or other rhythmic tool and begin to set a new, more powerful rhythm. Let it flow through you as you and your spirit or spirit-kin animal partner begin an internal interweaving. You may find yourself swaying, rocking, or even standing and moving gently. Everything is in flow. Let your humming fade as the rhythmic sound takes over. Then begin to inhale "Ah" and exhale "Ha" intensely, over and over, in sync with the rhythmic sound. As the power builds and the energy swirls around, you and your spirit or spirit-kin animal will be as one and the tablet will be blessed and centered.

When everything begins to become calm and focus, slow the rhythmic sound and let your vibrating sounds again become a calm humming sequence that eventually fades to silence. See and feel the spirit world fade as well. Visualize your spirit partner sitting (nesting?) on your spirit tablet, forging a deeper connection as your tools, talismans, and shrine settle into a truth that is real.

When all feels calm, open your arms and gather in the sphere of light. Let it fill you and settle in your heart center. As you and your spirit-kin animal hum together, images and thoughts and information will flow for a time, until all settles and becomes calm. When you both agree that it is time to end, sprinkle some of the natural water about and clap three times, making the cry of your spirit partner with each clap. Place your hands on the tablet and intone "Maaaa," as all the excess energy flows down into the Earth Mother, the root of all. Then place the new leaf on the spirit talisman, bow, and vibrate "Pa Tan He Ya!"

Scatter the offerings you brought for the animals and spirits, and record everything you experienced in your journal.

CHAPTER 8

UNLEASHING YOUR ANIMAL SELF

The underlying key to successful feral magick is unleashing your animal self, your inner primal spirit. You have to let go of your modern Western programming and accept the feral animal being you truly are deep down. You have to accept that you are an animal—as we all are. You have to break free from the chains of civilization and shed the blinders that were placed upon you as a child. Remember, we contain all the DNA of every animal on the planet; all creatures came from the very first DNA. This is the core of our animal self. Every animal is within us.

This means suppressing your conscious mind and quieting your ego so that your primal animal self can emerge from your deep unconscious mind where it has always been. This moves your ego-chattering consciousness into the calm, animalistic—and much more ancient—primal brain that is a vestigial part of our human evolution—what Carl Sagan refers to as "the reptile brain." When you move your consciousness into primal-brain mode and quiet your endlessly active ego-mind, you enter a new, more primal, state of consciousness—your animal self. You leave behind the myopic hyperactive person trapped in the endless chattering of your ego-mind and can intentionally return to being what you have always been—a feral animal.

Carl Sagan warns us of the conflict in his book *Cosmos*:

> Deep inside the skull of every one of us there is . . . the limbic system or mammalian brain, which evolved tens of millions of years ago in ancestors who were mammals, but not yet primates. . . . On the outside, living in uneasy truce with the more primitive brain beneath, is the cerebral cortex; civilization is a product of the cerebral cortex.

When you unleash your animal self, you move away from the conditioning of civilization and closer to your earlier ancestral relatives who worked with nature spirits. In this primal, liminal state, you can more readily be part of the vital animated world of nature and become coequal with all the creatures and spirits that inhabit it. In this state, you can work with animal spirits as equals.

Return to Feral Magick

Once you have begun to move deeper into the Animist world of your ancestors, make a regular habit of returning to walk and meditate in wild nature and get to know and work with the spirits that inhabit that primal, natural world. Wander the woods; explore all kinds of wilderness areas; spend time on beaches or in parks. Reach out to the spirits you find there. You may already have felt a spirit-kin animal hovering over your life—a crow, a fox, a deer. What does it feel like?

When you were a child, your open and imaginative acceptance of these animalistic spirits seemed completely natural. When you were a toddler, all things were wondrous. You could speak to trees and squirrels and birds, and they "spoke" back to you. And that is the world to which you are slowly returning. You are becoming a feral child again—a being as open and joyful and full of wonder as your wild child self was. The goal of feral magick is, essentially, to return to a state of consciousness that reveals the Neo-Animist world—the world that your toddler self experienced so long ago, and that many tribal cultures still experience today.

There are various practices that can help you become open to the world of nature spirits. This is a brief introduction to the practices we explore in this section. In one practice, you enter a light trance state that helps you break through your cultural programming and shift your reality framework. This makes it easier for you to accept the truth that you are indeed an animal, despite what you have been led to believe. When you enter a light trance, you open to your deep unconscious mind and embrace your primal being as your animal self. In this state of feral consciousness, you can more easily communicate with nature spirits, and especially spirit-kin animals. This can be done any time you go walking in nature as you open your mind to this simple practice.

Another practice found in many cultures is the belief that physical or mental "crossroads" represent the intersection between the mundane world and the world of the spirits. Any time you go walking in nature with your mind open, be aware of any crossroads you may come across. When you find one, take the time to stand or sit with it. Contemplate all that the crossroads means and the power of nature that it indicates.

The final practice is based on the principle that it is useful to open to all spirit-kin animals to widen your primal perceptions and enhance your liminal vision of their world, as shamans do, before opening to and possibly bonding with the spirit-kin animal that may be drawn to you. Some spirit-kin animals will simply observe you out of curiosity or politely check you out. But some may come closer and show real intuitive interest in you. As you go walking in nature you can open your mind to all the living creatures around you using all your senses. Then relax your senses and become open to the spirit-kin animals that may be about you. Your experiences may be subtle, but it is a good start.

Finally, all of these simple practices can be expanded intensely by learning how to open and shift into your animal self. Once you unleash your animal self and are accepted as a safe feral creature, all of nature will become more open to you.

Becoming Your Animal Self Rite

You will likely find this practice to be a very relaxing therapeutic experience that brings you to a deeply relaxing liminal state in which you get to enjoy a simpler, calm mental reality.

Find a place outside in nature—the wilder, the better—where you can avoid people. Find a place with trees where you can be alone, so you don't have to worry about others watching or interrupting you. This is best done at twilight or in the late afternoon or evening. Some prefer to work at night, if it is safe. Plan to spend thirty minutes with this practice, although it may last longer as you become more proficient. Bring along some pure water to drink, and some food offerings that are safe for animals—nuts, seeds, berries, or other simple items. Wear loose clothing—as little as possible or even none at all, if possible.

Be sure not to talk and try not to think once you begin the practice, because the interconnected centers of the brain are activated by language, and even by thoughts formulated in coherent language structures. Before beginning, identify some animalistic, nonverbal sounds that feel right to you—howling, growling, barking, hooting, etc. (I'm a fan of howling, myself.) Practice "rumbling"—growling deep down in your chest with your mouth closed. Use this like meditation. It can help awaken your animal self and induce trance.

Gently swaying or rocking forward and back while rumbling or making other animalistic sounds can help you sink into a more primal state and intensify the focus of the trance. Inhale while rocking back, as you visualize raising your animal self from your deep unconscious mind. Exhale when rocking forward while rumbling or growling or making other primal sounds that come naturally. Gently massage your fire chakra (located below your belly button); the Fire-Gut center. Called the Dan-Tien in tai chi, the fire chakra is the power center in your lower gut and it is a key to this practice. As you rub this center, visualize expanding, flaming energy filling and releasing your animal self. Visualize yourself changing and shifting into a more primal you.

When you feel this shift, enter a spot in the natural area you have chosen. Sit or stand and meditate deeply on the kind of wild, primal animal self you really are, deep down. Think about the animal noises you are comfortable making. Get comfortable and begin rocking and making animalistic sounds to encourage your animal self to arise. It may be disconcerting, wild, unusual; go with it. Let your ego and sense of self fade. With each forward rocking motion, raise your claws and roar or growl. Feel the animal self within you rise up and fill your being as your normal mind shuts down and begins to sink down into the darkness of your unconscious mind. Breathe, stretch. Let your animal self take over your feral body.

As you go deeper into a liminal state, lunge forward with your claws up and make the animalistic sound of your choice to the four directions and loudest in the center. As you do so, visualize all other creatures being a bit scared, but also interested. Tense your whole body, and emotionally and spiritually center your being and the area around you with your roaring.

Touch the earth with both your hands, feeling them sink deep into the earth. Deeply growl, caw, howl, or make whatever primal sound erupts from your animal. Doing so honors the Earth Mother and your animal self. Vibrate "Maaaaa, Maaaaa, Maaaaa," and end with a primal sound.

Take your time and relax now. Your frenetic ego-mind has mostly shut down as your normal human ego sinks further down, your feral animal self fully arises, and a more primal consciousness takes over. Focus on the fiery energy filling your animal-self being with warmth and energy as you become a more feral creature. Let your imagination flow as the wild, intense, and fiery aura is fully felt and seen clearly as a more primal, aware, present being.

When ready:

Rock forward and back to accelerate this shift and bring your primal feelings into sharper focus. When you feel ready, touch the earth with your paws and will the Earth Mother to fill you with power, while rumbling "Maaaaaaaaaaa Aha" three times. Breathe in the green earth energy, feeding your animal self. With your eyes closed, reach your claws out to either side and feel the power of the forest trees and the plants all about you. Breathe in deeply and fill yourself with the green energy of the woods as you rumble "Haaaaaaaaaaaaa Aha" three times. Feel the energy!

Next, reach up and feel the powers of the sky, the stars, the moon or the sun, and the cosmos above you. With your paws in the air, reach up and rumble and vibrate "Laaaaaaaaaaaaa Aha." Breathe in deeply! Let the celestial powers fill and clarify your animal self.

Now stand and begin swaying while uttering your primal animal sound. You are now in a full animal-self trance. Your primal self is finally released and one with the power of nature. Turn around and embrace the pure power and energy flowing about you. Really see the energies flowing through the trees and the earth! Breathe it all in! As a feral animal being, you can now see all things as vibrant and alive. Your reality has completely shifted, as have you. You are now part of the Other.

Slowly begin to walk in a circle and let your being fill with amazement. Use all your senses and marvel at the newness of it. You may begin to see traces or energy forms of the nature spirits. Commune with the trees. Feel the embrace of nature. You are being accepted as a fellow animal. Lie down and let it all fill you. Be mentally silent, and just accept.

When you are ready to end the rite, stand and pick up the container of water you brought. Begin swaying and rumbling again, and raise your paws to the sky as you honor the cosmos by vibrating "Laaaaaaaaaaaaaa Aha." Pour some water on the ground and feel the beginning of your animal self sinking back into your deep unconscious mind. Then reach out with your paws to the green trees and plants around you. As you sway and rumble, honor the great green plant beings and vibrate "Haaaaaaaaaaaaaa Aha."

Pour some water on the ground and feel your animal self sinking down further into your deep inner primal "dragon mind." Finally, reach out with your paws and place them upon the Earth Mother as you sway and rumble, honoring Gaia by vibrating "Maaaaaaaaaaa Aha." Let your feelings and thanks flow into the Earth. Pour more water on the ground. Sit for a time. Feel and "see" your animal self sinking farther back into your deep mind. Down, down, down. Feel it let go as the fire energy retreats into your lower belly and your human ego self slowly arises and resumes control of your mind. As this happens, stand and rock forward and back while inhaling and exhaling as before, until the transformation is complete.

Scatter the food offerings you brought for the spirits clockwise around you and silently thank them all. Let go of your vision of your primal self, but do not forget it. Drink some water and spill what's left on the earth.

You may end in silence, song, humming, or with any animal cry that comes to you—maybe a howl, a roar, a caw—as a final salutation from your animal self. Walk in silence from the woods. When you get home, stay silent, and record or draw your experiences in your journal. Be sure to pay attention to your dreams.

I recommend doing this practice often and then monthly so as to become comfortable with your feral nature and more open to all the nature spirits. Full moons are always the best time.

PRACTICE

Crossroads Walking Exercise

Do this exercise in a favorite natural place where you can relax. Bring some water, a small bag of seeds, nuts, or berries, and perhaps a small cloth to sit on.

Hike for a time. Be silent and completely open to nature until you come across a crossroads along the trail you are on. In this lovely wooded green place, find a spot where you can sit without being disturbed. Meditate on the intersection of the world of nature spirits and the mundane world of human reality. Once you have opened your consciousness to this sacred crossroads, stand within it and then stroll down the path you've chosen for a time. Open all your senses and hum a simple sequence that helps you enter a liminal trance state.

When you come to another place where two paths cross—a place that feels special, or perhaps even unreal—stop there. If you are comfortable doing so, sit in the center of this intersection. Breathe deeply and slowly. Close your eyes slightly—not all the way—and let your vision go out of focus. Where you stand now is again in the Other, within the world of nature, intersecting the world of human civilization. Focus more on being in a liminal "gateway." As you stand there, you stand with one foot in each world. You know the mundane world well, but now you are becoming more familiar with the world of nature spirits. Open your mind and your imagination to this task. Let the crossroads become your immediate world for a time.

Continue to breathe deeply. Hum, rumble, or make any animal sounds that come to you. Relax your whole body and quiet the constant chattering of your mind. Instead of thinking deeply, open your mind to the crossroads, the four directions, and all your senses as the nature spirits whisper to you in the rustling of leaves, the sighing of the wind, and the singing of birds. Let yourself focus on the patterns and details in the greenery. Touch and then smell the earth in the center of the crossroads. As you listen to the birds and breezes and chittering animals, close your eyes, and open your mind to what they are communicating. What images do they bring to you?

Breathe deeply and slowly until you are completely calm. Know that you are at the intersection of the two worlds. Place your hands on your chest and "see" the brilliant light of your primal spirit glowing. Open your arms and see the light expanding into a brilliant sphere all around you. Open your eyes a little, out of focus a bit. Be open to seeing the flashes or images that indicate nature or animal spirits are interested in you. Focus on any that call to you and commune with them.

Let your mind remain empty and open, and just wait. Wait for the sounds of nature to shift or speak to you in some way. Pay attention to your body, your feelings. Do you feel a chill or a shiver? A presence?

If a spirit-kin animal is present, relax and focus your eyes slightly. "See" that spirit-kin animal before you as a shimmer or swirl, or as an image, or maybe something else. Perhaps you see it flitter or glow among the trees. If you only sense or feel it, silently *ask* it to manifest in a perceptible form.

Does something glimmer there? Does a shadow shift? Do you hear an animal's cry? You may have sensed a spirit presence. If so, close your eyes and open your mind and your heart to this spirit. Here at the crossroads, at the intersection of two worlds, you can reach more easily into the world of nature spirits. You can crack open the gateway into the Otherworld. When you do, you make it clear to the animal or nature spirits that you are reaching out to them and that you are ready to have them reach out to you. This is an ancient but simple way to open to the Otherworld of the spirits.

Try this practice at different crossroads at different times to reach out to different kinds of spirits. Do what feels right, or simply do what you did before. Let the spirits help you, inform you, guide you. Trust your own instinct, intuition, and your insight. There is no one right way. Just follow your heart—and the spirits of nature.

PRACTICE

Opening to Spirit-Kin Animals

This practice can be done at midday or at twilight. As you did for the previous practice, find a lovely place in nature where you can be alone—preferably at a crossroads. Bring along a container of water and a small vessel that contains seeds, nuts, and/or berries. Bring a medium-sized blanket made from natural cloth to sit on. (White or green is best, but you can use any color that feels appropriate.) You'll also need two small twigs from two different trees that feel right to you—one with leaves, another with needles. Be sure to honor the trees before you take the twigs and thank them by placing your hands on them and communing with the spirit of each one. Then honor them with a small offering of water.

Once you have found the right place, lay out the cloth or blanket, sit down on it, and place the twigs in front of you. It is best to face east, but not absolutely necessary. Calm yourself by breathing deeply, then sink silently into a light trance state. When you are ready, clap three times to free the area of any negativity, then open your primal spirit by placing your hands on your chest and seeing the light of your spirit self glow. Open your arms and see the light expand into a sphere of light that surrounds you. Place both your hands on the earth, really feeling its power beneath you. Honor and awaken the Earth Mother with your own words or by humming a simple tune, then continue to honor her by vibrating "Maaaaa." Sit and be open to the world of spirits and meditate in that liminal space for a time.

When you are ready, pick up the two twigs, one in each hand, and place them in an "X" on the cloth before you. Quietly vibrate "Maaaa" three times as the energy from the earth rises into you to support the work you are doing. Feel this glowing power fill you as your breathing deepens. Then pick up the twigs and open your arms and vibrate "Yahh Ahh" three times to call to the spirit-kin animals. Hum a sequence that fills you, or a sing soft song to call the spirit-kin animals. Sway as you do so and empty your mind of all thoughts and worries, and open yourself to the energies flowing about you.

Close your eyes and cross the twigs over your heart, then begin whispering "Yahh Ahh" over and over, slower, and slower, while lovingly inviting all the spirit-kin animals to come. To extend this welcome, whistle in a scale that rises from a low to a high pitch, returning to a long, low note. Repeat this softly three times. (If you don't know how to whistle, you can bring a whistle with you—preferably a wooden one—or you can clap.) Wait in silence for a time until you hear something that indicates you have been heard—the cry of a bird or some other natural sound.

With your eyes partly closed and slightly out of focus, whistle or hum a tune that feels intuitively right for you. Start with a mid-level tone, then go up a tone, then down to a lower tone, ending on a tone that is slightly higher than before. Repeat this pattern slowly until you feel the spirit world gently opening around you.

When you sense, see, or feel the gathering presence of all the nature spirits and spirit-kin animals, open your arms with your palms facing up and, with your eyes remaining unfocused, continue to whistle the simple tune. As you do so, greet the spirit-kin animals with your love and your will and your heartfelt welcome. When one or more approaches your open palms, slow and soften your whistling and let it fade into silence. Take a deep breath and hold it, then breathe out slowly. Repeat this breathing and focus on what is happening around you without thinking.

Open your mind and see which spirits come. You may simply see ripples in the air or flashes of light, or you may feel something or hear soft noises. All of these responses are excellent proof that one or more spirits are responding to your call. As you go deeper into your light trance state, be aware of which spirits come, and be open to different feelings or visions without thinking deeply. If you sense that a specific spirit-kin animal—or perhaps more than one—is curious about you, begin your simple whistling or humming pattern again and radiate love and openness. Then see and feel and be open to what happens.

If a specific spirit-kin animal does approach you, cup your hands together to indicate that you want to connect and open your mind to that spirit, especially if you get a very clear vision and or an intense feeling. Close your eyes and see if an image or symbol or color appears in your mind's eye. If it does, offer that spirit love and interest and happiness. Send it greetings and remember the image and feeling you sense. Whether you bond with this spirit again or not, this is an auspicious moment for you both. You may even already have a bond.

When you are ready to end the encounter, vibrate "Yahh Ahh ha" three times with a rising tone and wide-open arms to let the spirits know it is time to go. Any spirit-kin animals you have encountered may seek you out in the future—perhaps at your home. As you prepare to end the rite, open your mind, and send out the thought that you are open to meeting other spirits. Then bow and honor the spirits by leaving the two crossed twigs on the earth before you as an offering for them and for the

Earth Mother. Scatter the seeds and nuts and berries you brought in a circle as an offering for both the spirits and for the animals they embody. Do this with gratitude, while vibrating a long soft "Ahh Haa YaaAA" with a lowering tone three times. Pour out the water.

Finally, open your arms and gather your primal spirit light sphere with your hands, returning all the light around you to your heart and body. Then touch the earth with both hands and give it all to the Earth Mother with a long "Maaaaa." Stand, clap your hands, say "Aha," then go.

CHAPTER 9

DISCOVERING THE GENIUS LOCI

As we mentioned in chapter 4, the genius loci is a powerful nature spirit that inhabits and centers a certain place within a special natural area or biome—maybe a pine forest, a particular wooded lake, or a swamp area, for example. All of these natural areas have their own flora and fauna and their own interwoven ecosystems, and the genius loci is the potent spirit center point. When you want to connect with the strongest and most helpful nature spirit of any wild area, seek out the genius loci. In fact, it makes perfect sense that, when trying to access the spirits of a natural place, you would reach out to the most potent or sacred spirit of that wilderness in order to get to know the spirit-kin animals that live there. Nothing will help you more with your spirit-kin animal work than the genius loci of a place, which can be considered the "taproot" of the spirit of the Earth. The next two practices will guide you in this work. The first will help you identify the genius loci of a place using your senses and your intuition. The second will help you connect with the animal spirits you will find within that sacred place.

PRACTICE

Finding and Honoring the Genius Loci

Find an open, natural, and healthy wild wooded area that feels sacred to you and wander through it as you have done in previous practices.

Bring water and some seeds, nuts, or berries as offerings. Relax and open your personal spirit-self light using the techniques described in the last chapters. Once you do so, hum a sequence that feels right and focus your intent on finding the powerful genius loci spirit and its place in that area.

Once you have entered a calm, liminal state, stroll through the area intuitively until you come upon a place that feels powerful and right to you—maybe a crossroads or a special stone, tree, or mound that calls to you. Stand or sit in silence there, and close your eyes. Breathe in deeply to a count of seven. Hold your breath for a count of seven. Then exhale for a count of seven. Repeat this process as many times as feels right to you as you relax your mind and body and let them connect to nature. Consciously breathe in the healing air of this lovely wild place as you open your mind and heart to it. Is this the right place?

Place your hands over your heart as you continue to breathe deeply, and "see" the light of your primal spirit glowing. Further extend this light into this powerful area all around you. As you enter a light trance, *feel* this place and the life that surrounds you and pulses above and beneath you. Listen to the sounds; smell the delightful scents of nature. Immerse yourself in the wind and the sunlight and the spirits around you. Open all your senses to the wonders of this place, but keep your eyes closed. Be still and open and loving to the nature spirits and spirit-kin animals who are interested in what you are doing.

Extend your hands palms up and project a bright ray of your spirit light out into the powerful natural place that attracted you. Focus intently, with strong will and love, on calling to the genius loci of the natural place that surrounds you. As you focus, repeat a simple humming sequence that feels right for this work. It may take a few tries to find one that feels right, but your spirit will guide you. A simple alternation between higher and lower tones often works for me.

As you hum, focus intently on your desire to call to the genius loci, the "guardian spirit" of this place. As you settle into a more focused trance, be aware that your ray of light moves like a compass needle.

With your eyes half-open and a bit out of focus, follow the direction of the light ray as it points you toward this mighty spirit. Once you get a sense of the direction in which to go, touch the earth and ask to be led to this mighty spirit. As you continue humming, focus on your ray of light and begin to walk slowly toward the genius loci, following your senses and your intuition. With every step, you move closer to this sacred place and begin to feel accepted there as one who honors and loves nature and its spirits.

As you walk, you may feel yourself being pulled to a specific place. If this happens, just stop and close your eyes. The ray of your spirit light will keep you on the right path and you will feel the pull of the genius loci. Keep your mind, heart, and body open to the connection you feel. When you begin to sense that you have arrived at the brightest and most powerful source of spirit energy, you will know that you have found the genius loci—the key nature spirit who grounds and centers this whole area.

When you find the genius loci, you will know. It will be set apart in some way. It will be vibrant and powerful. It may be physically rooted in a specific large stone, or a very old tree, or a mound, or something else that is clearly potent and special. It may reside in a spring or a pool, or in another very special body of water. No matter what or where it is, it will feel very powerful and, if you close your eyes slightly, it may seem to glow. Others may have left offerings there—a flower or a stack of stones is common. Stand or sit before this great spirit with your eyes closed and your arms open. With silent intensity, bow and honor the spirit with your own glowing spirit light that is shining from your heart. Begin humming again and open your being to the spirit of this place. Then wait for a contact, a sign, or an omen—the song of a bird, the cry of an animal, a creaking branch, or a sudden breeze. This is how you will know that you are welcome here.

As you sit or stand facing the genius loci, pour out some pure water and offer it seeds, nuts, or berries. Bow and whisper "Aaha Yah Ah" three times with your hands open and your palms facing up in a gesture of gratitude and openness. Speak other words or make animalistic cries as you feel is right. Whatever inspires you. Place both hands near or on the center of the home of this intense spirit and project your openness and love onto it. Close your eyes and sense the energy that radiates from this deeply rooted ancient spirit. Breathe, hum, and open fully to this powerful being, and wait for it to respond in a positive way. This response may come as images in your mind, as whispers you hear, as deep feelings you sense, or in many other ways.

When you feel that your presence has been acknowledged, ask for guidance and mentoring from the spirit. When you are ready to end, stand and bow while vibrating "Aaha Yah" three times. Finally, offer the spirit pure water or natural food items, or leave a small personal gift like a lock of your hair or something else that that feels right.

You and the genius loci are now connected and, if all went well, this powerful spirit will help you. Leave when you are ready, with the understanding that you may return as needed. This may become a regular place for you to do Neo-Animist workings. Be sure to record your experience in your journal.

PRACTICE

Return to the Genius Loci to Sense Spirit-Kin Animals

Once you have become comfortable within the power zone of the genius loci you found, you will be able to easily return to it and sense and better perceive the presence of many nature spirits as they gather around this place, suffused with energy. If you return to connect specifically with spirit-kin animals, follow the same steps you used in the previous exercise.

This time, focus on humming a lower-pitched pattern of tones as you open and embrace the energy and loveliness of the genius loci while also opening yourself to spirit-kin animals. Slip into a trance state as you hum, and you'll begin to feel and sense the many spirits gathering about the genius loci—including many spirit-kin animals.

Close your eyes slightly and let them go a bit out of focus as you have done before and continue deep humming sequences. You may sense or even see presences or flashes of spirit energy. Continue humming and offer a little water or food to these spirits, then bow and as you like ask the genius loci to help you commune with the spirits that may be right for you. Open your arms to those who approach you, but be sure to honor them all. If any spirit-kin animal is drawn to your energy, let it come. You may connect with one or more this time, and perhaps others at other times. The genius loci will help guide you through this process, so be open and patient. When you work with a genius loci, you can be sure that it will help you, maybe to connect you with a spirit-kin animal that is drawn to you, but don't be impatient. Take the time to immerse yourself and enjoy the magickal world you are in! The genius loci is a center of many things.

If you find that the genius loci directly communicates different humming patterns to you, try changing, humming patterns it teaches you, to be in sync with the pattern it suggests. This may offer many key ideas and useful ways to work with spirits. Remember them. A specific hum-pattern may signify that a specific spirit-kin animal is interested in connecting with you. Just close your eyes and see and/or feel the truth of this as you try humming the sequence the genius loci gives you; do so with joy.

Remember, just because a spirit-kin animal approaches you doesn't mean that it is one you will desire to seriously work with—and vice versa. All such relationships require time, consent, and the right connection. Every spirit-kin animal, just like every person, has its own way of perceiving, understanding, and working in the world. The complex world of spirit-kin animals is very different from our own. In fact, your spirit-kin animal partner may have been approaching you in some manner for a while but now you are able to be aware of it.

Once you have connected with a spirit-kin animal, take the time to meditate on the experience with an open heart and with gratitude. It may just be a nice meeting, or it may be a more serious bond. Remember to honor the benevolent support of the genius loci that made it possible. When you are done, stand with your arms open and vibrate "Ahh Yaa aha" slowly three or more times, pouring forth your thanks and love and gratitude. Bow and place your hands upon the earth and give honor to the genius loci and all the spirits with a final sequence of humming. Pour some water clockwise in a circle that encompasses the home of the genius loci and—with words, feelings, animalistic cries, songs, or humming—express your gratitude to these very powerful loving nature spirits and to the spirit-kin animals that acknowledged you. Then leave the rest of your offerings for all the spirits.

Finally, open your arms and pull all of the light of your primal spirit back into your heart. Offer just a little of this light to the genius loci with open, cupped hands, then cover your heart center again and "see" and feel a new light fill you—brighter and stronger than before. This is a gift from your new friend, the genius loci; let it empower you from now on. Place your hands on the earth and vibrate "Maaaa," returning all excess energy to the Earth Mother. Then go forth, perhaps whistling.

The genius loci can continue to be a very powerful spirit ally for you and offers a very strong place where you can do many kinds of feral magick work. The spirit world can be tricky, and at times a bit hallucinogenic, so be sure to remember where the place of the genius loci is and how to get there! Always remember to record this and your experiences in your journal.

CHAPTER 10

UNDERSTANDING SPIRIT-KIN ANIMALS

The term "animal spirit" has been common in New Age circles for many years, although it has often been used to mean "favorite animal" or "special animal omen." To clearly differentiate the idea used in this book I use an animistic term: spirit-kin animal. A spirit-kin animal means that animalistic spirits, spirit forms of animals, may have an affinity to you and you to them. Thus, they have a potential "spiritual familial" connection with you. Many who do divination with Animal Spirit cards use them to indicate a person's attributes, interests, or personality in terms of an animal spirit. They can also be used to indicate a love of a particular animal. Take me, for instance. I love otters and gorillas. I relate to them, and I feel my personality connects to them. But this is not a spirit-kin animal, an animal spirit that has autonomy. The spirit-kin animal that came to me and bonded to me, the one which I work with, is the wolf spirit. That is my kin and it was a bit of a surprise!

The term spirit-kin animal is more correct in the Neo-Animist context as it refers to animalistic spirits that take on powerful supernatural form. For example, as shamans say, a spirit bear has powers, intelligence, agency, and independence that a living black bear may not express. So understanding and working with spirit-kin animals as opposed to animals involves intense spiritual work. It entails accepting the belief that all things are alive—even transcendent spiritual beings like bear spirits.

As we saw in Part I, nature spirits in general—and spirit-kin animals in particular—were clearly part of ancient human belief systems. The acceptance and veneration of these spirits that arose in prehistoric Animist cultures are still taken quite seriously in many tribal cultures today. Shamanic practices, which include the ability to connect deeply with the natural world and the spirits that inhabit it, are hundreds of thousands of years old, yet still persist today. In this worldview, spirit-kin animals have agency and are potent powerful beings that must be honored and worked with carefully.

You may already have felt or encountered these nature spirits in some way, and may even have felt or been approached by a spirit-kin animal that was drawn to you in dream or meditation. If this is the case, you may already have begun to go deeper into the Neo-Animist world of spirits and now want to learn more about how to work with a spirit-kin animal that seeks a relationship with you. These ideas are what this chapter is all about.

In this chapter and the next, we'll look at the different ways in which animals and spirit-kin animals are related and how you can discover which animal spirits are interested in working with you. One way to go about that is by determining what I call the "orientation" of a spirit-kin animal, and we will look at that process more closely in chapter 11. In this chapter, I want to explore how you can learn more about different spirit-kin animals and just what it means to bond with them.

Investigating Spirit-Kin Animals

While it is true that your favorite animal is not often directly connected to your spirit-kin animals, it is also true that, if you do have a long-term intuitive connection with a specific animal, it may be a sign that an associated spirit-kin animal is drawn to you, and this feeling may be new to you. Spirits and otherworldly beings are not generally acknowledged in modern Western cultures, so the idea of reaching nature spirits may be something new for you.

In Neo-Animism, the spirit-kin animals and nature spirits are everywhere, and we share that world. You don't "hunt" for a nature spirit, or spirit-kin animal! Rather you open yourself to that world of spirits and honor them. They show you the spirit patterns of life, and some may reach out to you to form a relationship. In chapter 3, we discussed what it means to "sense" the spirits of the natural world and explore how these relationships can expand and empower your worldview. In chapter 4, we examined how you can use your instinct, your intuition, and your insight to connect with these spirits and how to gently open contact with them. In my experience, working in union with the nature spirits can bring healing, wonder, and wisdom because all of these have happened to me. I will be forever grateful to the wolf spirit who came and helped and guided me at a terrible, traumatic time in my life. We are bonded and have a deep relationship even now, which is how this book evolved.

A simple way to learn more about a spirit-kin animal like that is to meditate within nature and be open to specific animals that often come to you, especially in dreams and other liminal times—especially as a child—then to broaden your intuitive draw to that spirit-kin animal by studying the physical form of that animal and doing some research. The charts in chapter 11 can help you with that. By researching the physical living animal and the human beliefs associated with it, you can come to understand a lot about the spirit-kin animals that may be drawn to you as well. What deities and spirits have been associated with such animals across history? How has the role of that animal evolved over thousands of years? Answering questions like these will prompt instinctive and intuitive responses, and lead to "Aha!" moments of insight that may draw you to different spirit-kin animals as well.

This research can easily be done online and as your work evolves or changes it will help you understand more about the spirit-kin animal or animals that have been drawn to you. It may open up new feelings about a different spirit-kin animal, which may in turn evolve into a more meaningful interaction within the realm of nature spirits. The more information you learn about an animal, the deeper your potential relationship with a spirit-kin animal will be. You will also understand how and why they were held in awe by prehistoric humans and worshipped as powerful spirits and how, as such, many evolved into animalistic gods of the ancient world.

You can't understand the power of a spirit-kin animal by looking at animals in a zoo. Instead, it helps to understand how these animals came to be connected with spirits, gods, and goddesses, and that spirit-kin animal deities were honored for thousands of years and morphed into something transcendent. The jaguar spirit who often guides shamans in Central American ceremonies is, in many ways, the transcendent essence of all jaguars who ever lived.

These spirit-kin animals (or demigods) manifested in mysterious, spiritual ways through human veneration and rituals, and then evolved into conscious spirit beings, honored and worshipped as powerful primal beings because it was their will, and the will of humans, to become so. It was their fate, their destiny. Take some time as you read this chapter to contemplate this spiritual process.

We humans did not conjure up such animalistic spirits. Through our human-animal interactions, they evolved into powerful self-aware spirit-kin animals with agency, as do all living, conscious, spiritual beings. Remember, in an Animist world, all nature spirits have agency. When you step away from the Western mindset and begin to see all nature as alive, it is easier to understand how spirit-kin animals manifested and became conscious with their own wills.

The Neo-Animist worldview is a deep, but also very simple, way to see the world. And it is not found just in so-called "primitive" cultures. As discussed, the belief in nature spirits is very much alive in modern Japan. The fox spirit, found in many Inari-sama shrines, is an example of a spirit-kin animal that is taken very seriously in Japan and is honored everywhere. Many other cultures still work with these spirits as well. I urge you to keep an open mind as you begin your investigation of these spirits. Be sure to enter what you learn in the charts you will find in the next chapter.

Spiritual vs. Mundane Reality

In many ancient cultures, and even in modern cultures today, the difference between spiritual and mundane realities is often blurred or seen as interactional—that is, as two separate parts of one reality. Thus, in Neo-Animism, all things are seen as alive and "real" either in flesh or in spirit, but in very different ways. This is a view often taken in Eastern cultures. As you move forward in this adventure, I believe you will discover that these two realities are, in fact, integrated—that spirit-kin animals and physical animals are all part of one vibrant, interconnected natural world. As a lover of nature, you may already feel gentle nudges from the spirits that are quietly guiding you to this realization.

When a person in ancient times experienced a powerful awe-inspiring event, like a volcano erupting, it seemed reasonable to attribute it to a supernatural power—a living being that was clearly a powerful spirit. Even today, the sight of an active volcano elicits awe and a deep, reality-shaking inclination to believe that the event is the work of potent spiritual forces worthy of honor and worship. Natural events like these elicit awe, as does the belief in magickal spirit-kin animals and nature spirits. Powerful natural events or experiences have always elicited awe! This is why shrines I have seen all over the world honor the potent spirits of ponds and trees and mountains like Mount Fuji! This has led me to understand and then actually *feel* the reality of these spirits. In Japan, I discovered that most people not only believe in these spirits; they have often actually felt, seen, and encountered them. All my students in Tokyo believed in nature spirits!

While this Neo-Animist viewpoint falls outside the modern Western view of the world, I have found as I traveled that, in many countries, the world of nature and animal spirits is believed as very real. Moreover, the frightening environmental changes in our modern world and the possible destruction of our planet are waking people up to the ancient view that nature is an all-powerful reality woven together with ancient forces and spirits that are integrated with the earth and nature and may be watching us damaging the planet.

Yet we all embody all animals and share the same planet. Each of us contains the DNA of all the animals that have ever existed, from the distant past up until the present. We all come from a single-celled organism, and all living beings are united by the fact that we all came from the same source. When we connect with a particular animal or spirit-kin animal, we are actually connecting with an indwelling part of ourselves. And this also means that a part of us dwells within the animals that inhabit the natural world. So when you connect with a spirit-kin animal, you are bonding directly with a being that is already a part of you—the manifestation of your animal self. The practices below are grounded in this.

As you work with these practices, I believe you will feel a gentle nudge toward the reality of the spirit world—a world in which your spirit-kin animal awaits. As your viewpoint shifts and your mind opens, your own primal spirit will help you emerge into a world in which all is alive. Remember, you and all beings embody a primal spirit, and a primal simplicity lies at the core of the world. In the Neo-Animist world, all things are alive, and reality is an open, many-level, and flexible perception of the realm. This is the norm in most tribal cultures, folk magick, Paganism, heathenism, and the many other evolving magickal and spiritual practices. The animistic view still manifests as the ancient but ever-reviving practices of shamans, medicine men, mambos, and sorcerers. All these beliefs and practices emerged from the prehistoric origins of Animism.

As you work your way through these mysteries, sciences, and beliefs, it's also important to relax and let the animal information flow over and through you in a creative, meditative manner. Awaken and delight in your inner spirit and your feral self as the animal that you are. Be sure to record your experiences in your journal. Draw, paint, doodle, play music—all these things please and are encouraged by the spirits. All the spirits of nature, and spirit-kin animals in particular, are patiently waiting for you.

PRACTICE

Connecting with Your Spirit-Kin Animal through Study, Insight, Intuition, Instinct, and Imagination

Your imagination, deep inner "knowing," and will are key doorways to opening to and connecting with the right spirit-kin animal. By doing careful research and creating charts like the ones described in the next chapter, you become more focused and therefore more likely to call to the spirit-kin animal that desires to contact you. On a deep unconscious level, this begins to open the way for that animal spirit being to approach you. Your desire, your will, and your knowledge prompt your intuition, instinct, and your insight to create a genetic connection between you and a spirit-kin animal partner. In a sense, your thoughts and feelings may very well resonate with that spirit that seeks you. Working together in sync can form a bond and deep connection.

As your physical, intellectual, and spiritual focus sharpens and evolves, you may begin to feel or sense the presence of a spirit-kin animal that is drawn to you. Like being drawn to a person, this implies that your animal self is open to this communication and that the spirit-kin animal may be reaching out to you. Once you have researched the animal, its history and so on, felt it near you, and reached out to it using your instinct, insight, and intuition, it will be much easier for that spirit to open to you—to "break through" and touch you. Once that connection is made, you can begin to interact with each other, although this takes time and focus. This kind of evolving contact and spirit bonding has been experienced by shamans, Shinto priests, and others who work with spirits across time and across many cultures.

Once this relationship is established, it evolves very quickly. Soon you will begin the internal process of expanding that connection as the spirit-kin animal mentors and guides you, and you respond with respect and care. In my experience, this process begins with a very clear and stable image of the spirit, which develops into a growing internal, almost telepathic, exchange. Before long, the spirit may begin to interact with you in the "real" world, almost as if it were sitting on your shoulder. You will "see" the spirit in your mind's eye, as well as sense its presence. In fact, once you have opened the door to your spirit-kin animal, you may find that it has been waiting for you all along.

PRACTICE
Meditation, Dreams, and Journaling

Daily meditation can really help to move this process along. The kind of meditation you do is not crucial, as long as you take some time from your hectic life to meditate and open to the idea of connecting with a spirit-kin animal. When or if you begin to connect with nature spirits and even spirit-kin animals through meditation, even vague interactions strengthen communications. As your meditative focus expands, you will be able to work with spirits that come in dreams or visualizations and soon in a clear spiritual reality. In fact, there are thousands of myths and stories that tell of spirit-kin animals that have been honored as guides and helpers. Nature spirits and spirit-kin animals in general thrive on attention, positive interaction, and kindness—just as we all do. As in any relationship, communication broadens and deepens that connection. When you reach out through meditation, dreams, and silent contemplation, you sharpen your focus and open the door to these interactions more widely.

And this can happen quickly if you increase your contact with your meditative outreach. Drawing or writing when connected with tentative spirits or spirit-kin animals can begin to open a two-way communication and a tentative exchange of information. Images and symbols will begin to flow between you as the spirits learn about you and mentor you. These can be powerful and enhancing experiences that will lead to powerful relationships.

Dreams can also help to facilitate deeper bonding with your nature spirits and especially a spirit-kin animal pal. Many esoteric practices view *dreamtime* as a sacred spiritual place where the spirits and those who seek to work with them can interact. Dreamtime is a place where the spirits can easily connect with you and vice versa. If you have a spirit-kin animal interested in you, it may call to you in your dreams. If so, open to your own primal spirit while lying in bed before sleep and ask it to accompany you as you fall asleep. You can expand this interaction by asking the spirit to show you a symbol or an image that conveys an important message. Over time, reaching out to the spirits in your dreams can become a very effective way to deepen your interaction that will often bleed over into the waking world. Be sure to draw and write everything you can remember about your experiences in your journal when you awaken.

CHAPTER 11

CLASSIFYING SACRED ANIMALS

In the world of biological science, animals are classified by their genetic propensities and similarities, as well as by their habitat, their physical attributes, their relationships to each other, and their behaviors. In this chapter, we will put aside some of these more complicated structures and focus more on simple distinctions between the animals with which people identify today and the spirits they embody. We'll look at the attributes of several common animals and then look at ways you can use that information to identify and connect with your own spirit partner. Of course, you can research other animals and honored animals not mentioned here. This is just a sampling, not an exhaustive list.

Our planet is home to thousands of different animals that inhabit a broad range of environments. And each embodies a unique animal spirit. Here we will concentrate on how these different animals and their spiritual orientation relates to Neo-Animism and the practice of feral magick.

Sacred Animal Classifications

This is a very straightforward exploration about physical animals, their characteristics, and their unique intelligences, aspects, and skills. Deepening your learning and understanding about several animals will open deep instinct as to which kind of animal you are intuitively drawn to and which is drawn to you. This is not about "liking" an animal, but instead a way to open your primal animal self to recognize spirit-kin animals that may already be drawn to you and which you may be drawn to. Focusing on animals you're drawn to will lead the spirit-kin animals to be drawn to you.

To accomplish these goals, I have chosen various classifications of living animals, each with its own historical and biological characteristics, and each with its own spiritual history. What follows is just a sampling of some animals whose spiritual essences have been honored. They have been honored as both animals and sacred spirits or even gods in many ancient feral practices and worshipped as divinities in ancient times and cultures. As you work with the orientation charts that follow, you can reference the few example charts or use them as models to create your own unique animal-spirit "orientation chart" that can help you in your work understanding the sacred side of specific majestic animals.

Here are some common sacred animals you can explore:

- black bears and polar bears (*ursidae*)
- deer and moose (*cervids*)
- frogs (*amphibia*)
- otters and badgers (*mustelidae*)
- whales and sharks (*ichthyoids*)
- lions, tigers, and other big cats (*felidae*)
- ravens, crows, and hawks (*aves*)
- snakes and serpents (*reptilia*)
- wolves and foxes (*canidae*)

Of course, there are many other animals out there—for example, hyenas, elephants, horses, and primates, to name just a few. But, for our purposes here, we will limit ourselves to these nine.

Understanding the spirit orientation of each of these animal classifications can help to guide your work with a spirit-kin animal, although your own focus may be on a different animal. Using the template below, you can determine the spirit orientation for any animal you wish to study and approach.

As you investigate these animals and think on the spirit-kin animals they may embody, it is useful to contemplate their material forms as well as their spiritual forms and powers. When making decisions about how to work with them in feral magick, their physical as well as their spiritual and ritualistic characteristics can help you understand the deep personal connections you have with the animal powers in your life. Here, we will focus only briefly on biology and zoology, and then move into the spiritual realm.

You may feel a connection with one or more of the animals and their spirit forms in this list. But your intuitive spiritual connection to specific animals—and likely to spiritual animals as well—may emerge as something deeper than simply "liking" tigers or snakes or hawks. Being attracted to a specific animal is one thing; feeling an intuitive or psychic connection with its spirit-kin animal is something deeper. It indicates a spiritual resonance that involves your body, your heart, and your mind—a potent and intuitive bond—and that can help guide you in your work with the right spirit-kin animal. As you move forward, your primal animal self will help you join with and connect to your deep intuition about spirit-kin animals, and perhaps more. All of this will empower your feral magick work.

Spirit-kin animals have been a key part of shamans and their magickal techniques for thousands of years. We mentioned previously how your primal animal self and your prehistoric ability to work with nature spirits of all kinds have been suppressed by our current rigid cultural and societal beliefs. Yet Pagans, magick workers, and shamans from the dawn of time and across many cultures have acted as powerful helpers and guides, working with nature spirits and spirit-kin animals (sometimes referenced as "familiars") to heal, help, and understand the world. Some were persecuted or executed for practicing their powerful primal, natural feral magick. And around the world, especially in tribal cultures, working with nature spirits and spirit-kin animals persists most everywhere. The cultural programming that has blinded so many to their reality has begun to fall away. The ancient traditions and revival of feral magick are still with us.

Animal Spirit Orientation

Working with spirit-kin animals often involves mental images, dreams, and visions. And there's a lot that you can learn about a spirit-kin animal's body language by studying what the living animal does and why. That's why it is important to master key aspects of a physical animal's actions, sounds, and history in order to better understand the older, deeper, more powerful spirit-kin animal. This helps you develop the relationship you want to have with that spirit.

Below you will find a template example for summarizing and comprehending the spiritual orientation of an animal, as seen through its habitat, its behaviors, its history, and its associations. You can use this as a guide for researching and organizing the spiritual animals on which you decide to focus. This template can be a powerful tool for learning and processing information about animals, their powers, and their ancient associations, all of which can help you to connect them with their spiritual animal forms. The information you add to this template can help you understand important aspects of the animals you research and the relationship they may have to ancient deities and animal gods, as well as to primal spirit-kin animals. This, in turn, can help you better understand the animalistic spirits to which you may be drawn.

To help you understand and appreciate this process, I have also included four completed charts for four different animal classifications—wolves and other canids, crows and ravens, snakes and serpents, and lions and other big cats. These will give you ideas about how to coordinate your thoughts and feelings about the animals you are drawn to research, and help you think about their connected animalistic spirit forms—which are quite different from the living animals.

You can use the information you enter in this template to create your own animal-spirit "database" that can inform your work as you meditate on, contemplate, and begin to connect with the animal spirit on which you choose to focus. This will help you connect with physical and spiritual animals and lead you to the spirit-kin animals that may be drawn to you.

Animal Spirit Orientation Template (Example)

Animal:

Family:

Genus:

Species:

Habitat:

Description:

Behaviors and sounds:

History:

Associated deities and symbols:

Spirit orientation and integration:

Now let's look at sample completed templates for four different animal classifications. As you go through these charts, pay attention to how different animals and their associated animal spirits and deities unfolded over time. Then think about the spirit-kin animals or nature spirits that may have been attracted to you—the ones you intuitively feel have tremendous potential for your work. Consider the power such spirits can have to help you open to the Otherworld of the spirits.

Wolves and Other Canids

Family: *canidae*

Genus: *canis*

Species: *canis lupus*

Habitat: Gray wolves have a huge range, including all of North America, Europe, and parts of northern Asia. They thrive in many different ecosystems, including temperate forests, mountain ranges, rainforests, shorelines, mountains, tundras, grasslands, and deserts. This shows their adaptability.

Description: Wolves weigh between 100 and 120 pounds, stand two to four feet high, and generally measure five to seven feet long. They have fairly long legs and often broad skulls with a narrow muzzle. Some are larger than others. Their paws are large, four to six inches, with the forepaws being larger than the hind paws. Their tails are long and bushy and hang straight down. Their coats, which have a thick, dense underfur, vary by season. Colors vary from gray to dark gray with black-and-white sections, to brown, to solid black or solid white. They have upright flexible ears that are similar to those of a husky.

Behaviors and sounds: Wolves cooperate and work in groups when hunting game and are known for stalking and attacking as a pack. This lets them take down large prey. They have a social nature and very expressive behavior. They travel in nuclear families, often mate in pairs, and raise their offspring. They are territorial and will fight to defend their turf. They are both omnivorous and carnivorous. When they are alert or upset, they prick up their ears and bare their teeth. When their ears are back, it indicates they are suspicious, submissive, or threatened. When their ears are forward, they are attentive and listening. They may wag their tails, or they may tuck them between their legs or hold them erect. Sometimes they arch their backs; sometimes they either lounge or curl up in a posture called pack cuddling. They have a tendency to bare their teeth when threatened and as a warning. When lying down, they may be relaxed and submissive. They may also run, leap, or dodge while playing. Sounds include howling, growling, rumbling, barking, whining, and chuffing.

History: The worldwide wolf population is estimated at 300,000. Wolves have a long history of interactions with humans, but they have been feared and hunted because they attack livestock. They have been honored, worshipped, and respected in many tribal societies.

Associated deities and symbols:

Anubis or Golden Wolf (Egyptian), the god of the underworld who guides the dead and is thought to be a golden wolf, not a jackal.

Asena (Turkish), an ancestral she-wolf deity associated with the Göktürk foundation myth.

Chipiapoos (or Jiibayaabooz) (Native American), often seen as a wolf spirit and known in the Chippewa and Algonquin tribes, among others.

Fenrir (Norse), a massive wolf-deity, and the son of Loki who initiated Ragnarok, the "end of the world," during the final battle of the gods.

Garmr or *Garm* (Norse), a wolf god associated with Hel, goddess of the underworld.

Lupa (Roman), the divine she-wolf who saved and raised Romulus, the founder of Rome, and his brother Remus.

Lykos or *Lycaeus* (Greek), Lycos, Lycus (Greek), or later Lukos (Roman) means "wolf" or wolf deity. Several heroes were call by this name.

Mánagarmr or Moon Wolf (Norse), a divine wolf in Norse mythology. Described as a white arctic wolf connected with the moon.

Skoll or Sun Wolf (Norse), a wolf spirit mentioned in the Prose Edda. He chases the sun as it is ridden across the sky by the sun goddess.

Wepwawet (Egyptian), a god whose name means "opener of the way" to the underworld. Sometimes shown as a light grayish wolf riding the sun barque.

Crows and Ravens

Family: *corvidae*

Genus: *corvus*

Species: Various (crows, 34; ravens, 9)

Habitat: Crows can be found most anywhere in the world, ravens less so. Their habitats differ, although there are many similarities.

Description: The common raven (*corvus corax*) is between twenty-four and twenty-seven inches long and weighs around forty ounces. They prefer both mountainous and coastal areas far from human habitation. Crows are smaller, between sixteen and twenty-two inches long and about twenty ounces in weight. Some European crows are slightly larger than American crows and are often confused with ravens. Crows are more comfortable within city limits and have adapted well to people and urban settings.

Behaviors and sounds: Crows and ravens are often monogamous, and breeding partners can remain together for years. Crows form large family groups of up to fifteen, and older individuals often help raise the younger ones. Crows have the same brain-weight-to-body-size ratio as humans. Although crows do not have a neocortex like humans, they do have an area in the brain that is just as complex. Crows and ravens use and create tools and can solve complex problems. Some, like the Caledonian crow, are meta tool users, using one tool to acquire another to then solve a problem. This behavior indicates they are capable of an amazing degree of abstract thinking, and they have been known to pass on knowledge from one generation to another. They have imagination and can project at least three steps into the future. They remember faces and situations and have been known to bring small gifts to humans who have helped them. They are capable of deceit and engage in cheating, stealing, and trickery—for instance, secretly following another animal to discover a cache of food and then stealing it. They recognize the concept of fairness and, when they know they are being cheated, will shun the cheater. They have been known to build decoy nests during mating season when they feel that they have been spied upon. They play by themselves as well as with each other, sometimes as a learning strategy and sometimes just for fun. They can be fairly acrobatic in flight when they need to be, although they generally use a steady flapping motion and not too much gliding. Both crows and ravens are hunters as well as scavengers and will go after small reptiles and rodents as well as the young of other birds. Both of them attack raptors like hawks who hunt them. Ravens often go after crow eggs and their young. Although they are compatible, crossbreeding between ravens and crows in the wild is rare.

Both ravens and crows have a wide range of vocalizations, with crows using as many as twenty different calls. Most crows utter the familiar "caw caw caw" sound, while ravens utter a louder, throatier "kwak kwak." Both crows and ravens clack their beaks to communicate a variety of feelings, and both are excellent mimics. The family of *corvidae* are considered songbirds as well. Depending on the environmental context, a crow's cawing can mean many things—from a conversational greeting, to the sharing of information, to a warning about a threat. When scolding, they emit an extremely loud and fast series of cacophonous caws. When in more intimate communication with family and friends, they make soft rattling sounds and clicks. They have been known to talk to themselves, just like humans.

History: The folklore of crows and ravens seems to revolve around luck, fate, and trials or struggles. Even today, they are honored as being crafty, tricky, and intelligent. Traditionally, the crow spirit offers to bring mental and spiritual gifts that can sometimes be tricky or even blow up in your face. I find that they teach us to be humble. Most legends and stories center on the raven, but crows are far more common today. In fact, the mythic distinction between ravens and crows is blurry, and one is often confused with the other.

One of the names of the Norse god Odin is *HarHravn*, which means "high raven." He was known by his two raven familiars, *Hugin* (thought) and *Munin* (memory). Later lore of the region tells of the *Valravn*, ravens that become a supernatural force after eating the heart of a king or knight on the battlefield. They can become humans by eating babies as well. One tradition claimed that a raven banner brought soldiers luck in battle. Another claimed that, to invoke the spirits of ravens, you had to go to the mountains or the coast away from densely populated areas. Crow spirits, on the other hand, could be invoked in the city—although it was considered wise to feed the crow population nuts and honor them with other appropriate foods to create a bond. The raven is the national bird of Bhutan and its image sits upon the king's crown as a talismanic force of protection.

Associated deities and symbols:

> *Corone* (Greek), the familiar of the goddess Athena. A famous statue of Athena holding a crow in her outstretched hand stood in the town of Corone in Messenia in ancient Greece.

Dhumavati (Hindu), a goddess who can act as a bestower of boons and *siddhis* (magickal powers). She rides a wagon driven by a crow.

Kakasya (Buddhist, Tibetan), a guardian goddess known as a crow-aspected *dakini*, or magickal spirit.

Lycius (Greek), a raven spirit thought to belong to Apollo, whose name ironically means "wolflike." Lycius was originally a wealthy man who disobeyed Apollo and was turned into a white raven.

Mahakala (Buddhist, Hindu), a form of Shiva that is honored as a deity called *Kakamukha*, meaning "raven faced."

The Morrigan (Irish), the great queen who often roams the battlefield as a raven. Likewise, the war goddesses Babh and Neman appeared as hooded crows.

Nachtkrapp (German) or night raven, who appeared as a scary sort of bogeyman.

Ruha (Hindu), a raven god who was the lord of eclipse.

Shani (Hindu), a deity associated with Saturn who rides upon a crow.

Tengu (Japanese), a crow-headed and winged *yokai* spirit sometimes seen as a deity of the mountains. It has the body of a human, the head of a crow, wings, and claws instead of feet. They can offer wisdom and healing to those who honor them.

Crows and ravens were seen as potent beings and cultural heroes in many of the First Nations and tribes of North America. But they were also sometimes seen as benevolent tricksters. In several Pacific Northwest coastal tribes, including the Tlingit, the Bella Bella, and the Kwaka Kwaka, stories survive in which the raven acts as both trickster and creator. The Kwaka Kwaka call him Kwekwaxa'we.

Snakes and Serpents

Family: constrictors, venomous and nonvenomous snakes

Class: *reptilia*

Suborder: *serpentes*

Habitat: Snakes of various kinds are found most everywhere except in the Arctic and other extremely cold climates. The red spotted garter snake, the Puget Sound garter snake and other garter snakes, and the northern rubber boa are common in the Pacific Northwest. None are dangerous. The snake spirit is best contacted in areas where snakes live and have been seen, as well as in places where snake spirits were or are still venerated by native cultures. This includes special places that are associated with serpent images or icons, petroglyphs, or serpent earthworks like Serpent Mound in Ohio.

Behaviors and sounds: Snakes smell by flicking their tongues in and out. Although they sometimes appear to yawn, they are really just opening their mouths to "smell." They typically glide along the ground or in water or in trees with an undulating muscle movement, or by wriggling or moving from side to side, often in the shape of an "S." They shed their skins one or twice a year. When snakes retract their heads and coil themselves, it indicates a defensive posture and preparation to strike. Because snakes are cold-blooded, like all reptiles, they often seek warmth by curling up in a pile with other snakes. They hibernate in winter (called "brumation"). They fear people and grow angry when stared at. Their skins are not slimy, but dry. Some lay eggs; some give birth to live young; some hatch eggs inside their bodies. Many can climb trees and all snakes can swim. They can strike from almost any position. Snakes of different species are known for hissing, rattling, buzzing, growling, and even shrieking to warn off predators or approaching animals. Some shake their tails or rattle as a warning.

History: Snakes are an ancient species that evolved around 170 million years ago, likely from lizards around the Middle Jurassic period. The oldest snake was likely *eophis underwoodi*, a small snake that lived in what is now England. Today, snakes are found in various ecosystems around the world, including swamps, forests, deserts, woodlands, and grasslands. They can be found in both fresh and salt water. Some are nocturnal; others prefer daylight. Some are poisonous, although many are not. Most are predators and eat a wide variety of prey.

Associated deities and symbols:

A'yahos and *Sisiutl* (Pacific Northwest), serpent spirits honored by native tribes. The first is a serpent spirit that shakes the earth; the second is a two-headed spirit with a head at each end.

Caduceus (Greek), symbol of the god of healing associated with Asclepios, generally depicted as two serpents entwined around a staff. Other Greek deities like Hekate and Gaia were also associated with snakes.

Corra (Celtic), an oft-forgotten serpent goddess connected with fertility, the earth, and the image of two intertwined serpents.

Damballah, Blanc Dani, Mamo Wata (Afro-Caribbean), snake spirits honored in Vodou and other religions.

Lares (Roman), ancestor spirits that appeared as snakes.

Midgard Serpent and *Jormungand* (Norse), giant mythic snakes.

Nagas (India and Southeast Asia), spirits that can appear as giant snakes, half-human and half-snake, or all human. They are often associated with royal families.

Quetzalcoatl, and *Q'uq'umatz* (Aztec and Mayan), large snake spirits that could sometimes fly.

Rainbow serpent (Sutralia), snake spirit honored as the great divine creative power by Aboriginal cultures.

Wadjet, Renenutet, Nehebkau, Meretseger, and *Apep* (Egyptian), all serpent deities.

Lions and Big Cats

Domesticated cats are remarkably similar to large cats found in the wild. Here, we'll be describing lions and lionesses, but most cats are very similar in many ways.

Family: *felidae (felis)*

Genus: *panthera*

Species: *panthera leo*

Habitat: Lions live in African grasslands and savannahs, along with some other large cats. As pressures increase on these habitats, they are becoming rarer. Domesticated cats live just about everywhere. Some species of big cats can be found in Siberia and in jungle areas in Asia. Unfortunately, almost all these species are endangered due mostly to human destruction of their natural habitats.

Description: Both male and female lions are covered in fur. They are muscular and broad-chested, with long, tufted tails. Male lions, which are larger than lionesses, also have wide hairy manes. They are social and live in groups called prides that are made up of a few adult males and females, as well as cubs. Female lions socialize and hunt together, bringing down hooved animals like zebras and wildebeests. Lions hunt in the daytime, but can also do so at night.

Behaviors and sounds: Both sexes defend their territory by growling and roaring, which can sometimes be heard up to five miles away. They nudge each other's heads and bodies, and enjoy physical contact. When they are annoyed, they snarl with displeasure and slap with their paws. When they are happy, they make loud and deep purring and rumbling sounds, and sometimes moan, huff, or snort. Both males and females use their claws and teeth, and can fight to the death. Their claws are always kept sharp because they are retractable. They usually hunt every three to four days, often at night but sometimes during the day. They communicate and gather information through their sense of smell.

History: Lions were around as early as the Upper Paleolithic period, as shown in images on cave walls found at Lascaux and other ancient sites. Although lions are found primarily in Africa and India today, in ancient times they were found over much of the world. This is likely why images and symbols of them are so pervasive. Lions appear in most ancient and medieval cultures, and have been described or shown in art and literature from prehistoric times to the present. They were kept and honored, and sometimes worshipped, in Egyptian, Greek, and Roman times all over the world.

Associated deities and symbols:

Aion (Persian), a lion-headed god associated with the zodiac cycles. Also known as *Zervan*, this god was associated with mystery religions and Mithras.

Aker (Egyptian), a deity appearing as twin lions with a sun disc between them, one named *Duaj* ("yesterday") and the other named *Sefer* ("tomorrow").

Anhur (Egyptian), god of war called the "slayer of enemies." He was depicted as a lion-headed man with a beard, holding a spear or lance.

Anzu (Nubian), a lion-headed warrior god also known as *Apademak*.

Arensnuphis (Egyptian), lion-headed god whose name means "good companion." He was seen as the consort of the Egyptian goddess Isis.

Bast (Egyptian), goddess of the earliest domesticated cats in the world, from pre-dynastic Egypt. Also known as *Bastet*, she was associated with the moon, protection, sexuality, and much more. Cats were worshipped in ancient Egypt, and anyone who killed one was executed!

Haldi (Mesopotamian, Urarat/Ararat Kingdom), a warrior god also known as *Khaldi* who was depicted as a man with wings, standing on a lion.

Hercules (Greek), a demigod of strength and heroes who was a divine protector of mankind. He was depicted wearing a lion's skin because he defeated the Nemean lion.

Horus Her-Em-Akhet (Egyptian), god of the dawn portrayed as a sphinx, with the body of a lion and the head of a man. Known as *Harmakhis* in Greek.

Maahesm (Egyptian), ancient lion-headed god of war, protection, and weather.

Mithra (Persian), a popular and pervasive sun god often depicted as a lion who was worshipped throughout the ancient world over eons.

Narasingha (Hindu, Tantric), a lion-headed god of protection, destruction, yoga, and time. He banishes evil and fear.

Nefertum (Egypt), ancient god depicted as either a lion-headed or lotus-headed man who represented primal sunlight and the Egyptian blue lotus flower arising from primal waters.

Ninurta (Sumerian), ancient god of farming, healing, hunting, law, and war. He was shown as a beast with the body of a lion and the tail of a scorpion.

Nongsaba (Indian), lion god worshipped in the Meitei religion who took the form of a lion. His name means "one who made the sun" and also "all the light in the universe."

Ra (Egyptian), the most ancient Egyptian god of the sun, sometimes shown as a lion crowned with a sun disc. Also known as *Re*.

Sekhmet (Egyptian), great goddess who manifested Ra's power, the Eye of Ra. She was a mighty goddess of war, protection, and healing who was depicted as a lioness.

Shara (Mesopotamian), lion god who was responsible for agriculture, livestock, and irrigation, but was also a divine warrior. Shown as a lion or a god with a lion.

Tutu (Egyptian), god known as "the Lion" or "Great of Strength" who fought off demons and evil. He had the body of a winged lion and the head of a human.

PRACTICE

Creating an Animal Spirit Orientation Chart

Now that you have seen how descriptive and helpful these charts can be, you may be intuitively attracted to another animal or two. If so, create one that can help you discover if this approach leads you closer to your animal spirit of interest. Explore the information you find online and in print, and consider the interesting cultural and spiritual connections that have evolved around that animal. Take the time to do the research and think about what you find. Then create a similar chart that focuses on the animal (and animal spirit) to which you are drawn.

If unsure which animal to research, meditate on the animals that intuitively attract you along with their spiritual aspects. Then choose the one that feels closest to you.

You may realize that the animals you deeply *like* are different from the animal spirits you feel drawn to. If that is the case, try using the simple meditation below to help clarify this issue.

PRACTICE
Animal Spirit Meditation

This practice should be done outside, even if you're just sitting on a porch. It should be done once you have felt very strong connections with a possible spirit-kin animal. Have your journal and a pen handy, and bring along some pure water and some seeds, nuts, or berries to use as offerings.

When you are seated and comfortable, begin with a simple deep-breathing exercise. Breathe in deeply and silently to a count of seven, until you are completely relaxed, centered, and calm.

Visualize a glowing ball of bright light centered in your heart. This is your primal spirit. Place your hands together over your heart as the light glows brighter, then slowly open your arms and see a sphere of light form and expand all around you. This light will center and protect you. As you relax, breathe deeply, and let your awareness become open to all of nature—the earth and sky, and all the greenery around you. You are the center of all this.

As you breathe, quiet your mind and slip into a light trance or liminal space. Let your eyelids half close, and do not focus on anything at all. If you feel your eyelids closing, that is fine too. Then vibrate the sound "Ahhh" as you exhale and "Haaaa" as you inhale. Continue this as you relax and go deeper into a meditative state. In your mind, silently ask for the right animal spirit to come to you. Then just wait.

After a time, you may see or sense a light or odd flickering in front of or around you. Without trying hard, watch this energy as it flutters or moves. Exhale slowly while quietly vibrating "Ahhhh." Then inhale slowly while vibrating "Haaaa." Continue to watch or feel the energy with your eyes half closed and out of focus. If what you are sensing slowly resolves into an image or symbol, just let it happen. If it remains a feeling, relax into it. Open your mind and project love and caring.

If you sense that the presence is a spirit-kin animal you have been thinking about, begin to hum, alternating between high and low tones over and over—softly with love. If you sense that it is a spirit-kin animal that is attracted to you, open your palms in front of you. If the spirit comes closer, simply relax. Do not try to do anything; just hum and be open to it. Be aware that you are experiencing the world of the spirits. Continue your low, calm humming and remain relaxed as it opens to you.

Open your mind to any ideas, images, and feelings that may come to you from this being. It may turn out to be a different being than you expected. Simply remain calm and open, just as you would if a hummingbird hovered near you. If it is a spirit-kin animal, it may acknowledge you, and you can silently do the same. Keep in mind that it may be another kind of nature spirit that is called to you—a tree spirit or a river spirit. This just indicates that you have a connection with these beings as well. And that is very positive.

Be open to visions, whispers, and feelings during this first encounter. Hold the image of the animal spirit or other nature spirit clearly in your mind. Eventually, the form of the spirit will begin to fade, or it may simply flit away.

When this happens, open your hands and bow to the spirit, honoring it with love and light from your heart. As you do so, vibrate "Eeeee Ahhhh Oooooo" three times in descending tones as a warm parting. Then stand, bow to this spirit and to all the spirits, and honor the experience. Leave the food items you brought as an offering by sprinkling them on the grass or earth.

Touch the ground to honor the Earth Mother while vibrating "Maaaa" three times. Then hold your hands up with your eyes closed as a gesture of thanks. When you are ready to leave, open your arms and collect the sphere of light you projected and pull it back into your heart and being. "See" the sphere of light sink into your heart center, making you feel calm and full of peace. Then clap three times and cry out "Ahhh Yaa" three times as a farewell.

If only a faint echo of an animal spirit comes to you, simply repeat this meditative rite as often as you can. Better yet, take a walk through the woods and open yourself up to the realm of nature spirits while doing this same meditation and silently asking for the animal spirit that is right for you. The more often you access the potency of deep nature, the easier it will be for you to connect with the animal spirit that is attracted to you. The spirits themselves will let you know how to adjust this process to better connect with them.

This simple meditation will begin to consolidate the experiences that you have in nature and will help you open to the animal spirit you feel destined to work with. Pay attention to everything you sense and feel during this meditation and be sure to write it all down in your journal.

CHAPTER 12

EMBRACING YOUR SPIRIT-KIN ANIMAL

As we have seen, feral magick has its own set of rules and its own methods. But much of it is based on intuition and comes from your animal self. When you start to interact with the world of nature spirits, you rely on your own primal instincts. Your inner self guides you through intuitive insights that arise from your unconscious mind, not your intellect. In short, to embrace a spirit-kin animal, you have to connect with your animal self and become a bit more feral.

The process of embracing your spirit-kin animal begins with accessing the world of deep nature, something you have probably already experienced by this time (see chapter 2). If you have begun to feel or sense a spirit-kin animal that is drawn to you, there are many ways to gently nurture that feeling—and that's what this chapter is all about.

One key to forming a connection with a spirit-kin animal is to become aware of the inner attraction and intuition you feel toward it. This is not so much about the interest you may have in an animal as it is about recognizing a possible spiritual kinship. That may indicate why it's reaching out to you. You may not have been able to "see" or sense this spirit, or to really perceive it for a variety of reasons. But once you have opened to the world of spirit-kin animals, you will find that you are better able to connect with them—especially one that is attracted to you. After beginning to form this kind of consensual connection, you must decide if you want a more serious bonding. If you do, then it is time to go into the wildness and find a place of power in which you can create that deeper relationship. You'll find an exercise at the end of this chapter that can help you do that.

Meeting Your Spirit-Kin Animal Partner

There are lots of simple ways you can let a spirit-kin animal know that you want to connect. One feral friend of mine works directly with a crow spirit that helps guide and transform his life. When he connects to that spirit, he wears layered black clothing, a black coat that looks very much like the tail of a crow, and a black hat adorned with feathers the crows bring him. He carries peanuts as an offering to the crow spirit and to strengthen his bond with it. Actual crows know and recognize him, and bring him shiny things. He feeds them and speaks to them. When expressing emotion, he caws and clicks his teeth, turning his head sideways. He speaks with crows directly and has conversations with crow and raven spirits. They respect him and understand him and respond to him.

This is similar to my work with the wolf spirit, and I know others who work with spirit-kin animals in comparable ways. Many of us benefit from our use of feral magick and our contact with nature and animal spirits. Like the witches of old who were burned alive for having familiars that empowered and guided them, we are helped and protected by our spirit-kin animals. Fortunately, however, we no longer have to worry about being burned at the stake!

In my travels and firsthand experiences, I have found many who work with animals that are spirits. Siberian shamans I've met with honor many such spirits, and especially the bear spirit. In Japan, I have visited shrines that honor serpent spirits, fox spirits, turtle spirits, and wolf spirits. In Guatemala, I met with a group of shamans who performed a ritual that reached out to ancient Mayan gods and spirits, amidst shockingly powerful rites. In Oaxaca, I encountered shamans that especially honored the deer spirit. I have encountered feral magicians in the jungles of Southeast Asia and visited temples to snake spirits in Nepal. No matter where you find them, the veneration of animal spirits is real and powerful.

Once you have a clear idea about which spirit-kin animal is reaching out to you, you can work to connect with it whenever it feels right. Begin by opening up your primal spirit from your heart center and reaching out to the spirit-kin animal intuitively and emotionally. You can do this anytime and anywhere, but somewhere outside amidst nature works best. Remember to open your sphere of spirit light first to make sure you are in a safe space. Then follow your intuition and be open to the communication with the spirit.

As you awaken to your own spirit partner in this way, you will be honoring practices that are rooted in ancient beliefs and are still deeply embedded in many cultures and traditions today. When you rediscover this wisdom and embrace the spirits of nature, you start down a path that can lead you beyond the destructive forces of our dysfunctional modern world.

Walking the Path with a Spirit-Kin Partner

We all have a desire to connect with anything or anyone that can help and guide us in this life. Many of us have pets that we intuitively know will love and help support us emotionally, and sometimes even physically. Many of us collect animal images, or wear animal T-shirts, or buy and display animal items. These are all indications of a deep desire to reconnect with the animal spirit world and walk the spirit path.

Today, the urge to love and dream or fantasize about actually becoming an animal is growing. We see it in anime, in games, in role-playing, in furry gatherings, and more. This may be a growing indication that, as more animals become extinct, spirit-kin animals are breaking through to urge us to work directly with their powers. This is something I have been feeling myself, along with others who work with feral magick and spirit-kin animals. This is why I have written this book—to speak to those who are drawn to wildlife and maybe spirit-kin animals, and encourage them to connect intuitively to the spirit world around them.

When you connect with such spirits, it will change your life and your world. And most importantly, it will change you. As you walk the spirit path, you become wilder and more feral and more animalistic. You may alienate some, but you will be drawn to others who, like you, feel more alive in and part of nature and its spirits. Your senses can become more acute and you may find yourself reacting more strongly to pollution, and restrictions, and animal cruelty, and the toxicity of our civilized world. You may become a supporter of animal rights. You will become more feral and be happier as you become more connected with the natural world around you.

As I have worked with feral magick over the years, I have found that my loyalties have become somewhat divided. I certainly hope that our species survives and evolves in a way that stops the destruction of our planet. But a part of me has become more focused on the survival and empowerment of all animal species—especially those that are endangered. The more feral I become, the more I find the endangering of animals and the suffering of animal spirits deeply painful. If you feel this in some way, then you may already be walking the path of feral magick. You are already opening your animal self and are likely already drawing spirit-kin animals to you.

Here are some ways that you can enhance your intuitive connection to the world of such animalistic spirits.

- ✦ Change the way you dress and the colors and styles you wear. Use only cruelty-free products.

- ✦ Wear items that echo the spirit-kin animal to which you are drawn. Surround yourself with items that resonate with that spirit and adopt mannerisms that attract it.

- ✦ Try to avoid the pain and slaughter of animals and their spirits. I honor the bull or cow and their spirit, so I don't eat beef and I only eat some cruelty-free meat. I respect and honor the animals I eat and their spirits. My wolf spirit, for example, is okay with this.

- Study the animals that reflect the spirit-kin animal to which you are drawn. Watch videos of this animal; study them online; observe them in the wild or in cruelty-free zoos. Study their behaviors, their history, and their spiritual associations. When the wolf spirit first contacted me, I learned a lot about wolves from videos, online sites, and especially from books.

- As you begin to focus on your spirit-kin animal, work with it in your sacred places, best being in nature. Use your intuition to help you reach out. Make sure to take notes in your journal.

- Draw and create art that flows from this animal and your spirit-kin animal. Work in any way you like, with materials that call to you. Creating and working with spirit images, symbols, and sigils can be incredibly potent when engaging in feral magick, because it brings you and your spirit-kin animal closer.

- Decorate your home with items that resonate with your primal, feral self, with an emphasis on the spirit-kin animal that attracts and is attracted to you and the actual animal it reflects.

- Be receptive to items that may come from your spirit partner. Small gifts may arrive as you walk in nature, or your spirit-kin animal might leave small gifts on your balcony. Such "spirit gifts" may turn up unexpectedly in an antique store, or be sent by a friend. Some of these can be quite amazing. Once the wolf spirit and I became closer, friends started giving me images or items related to wolves, often without even knowing about my connection, and my online connections were suddenly filled with wolves.

Once you commit yourself to bonding with your spirit-kin animal, your whole world changes. As you spend time doing feral magick and making simple offerings to your spirit partner, it will work to spend more time with you.

The closer you and your animal partner become, the more your perceptions will shift and the more enhanced your senses will become—including your instincts, your intuition, and your insight. As I began working with the wolf spirit, I became much more intuitive about the people and things around me. My reflexes became more sharply honed. When I learned to "shapeshift" with and merge with the wolf spirit, I was shocked at some of the surprising yet intense ways this bonding changed my senses and my perceptions. (We'll talk more about shapeshifting in chapter 15.) When you let your spirit-kin animal connect to and transform you, it will lead you intuitively down an exciting spiritual path.

PRACTICE

Finding Your Place of Power

The goal of this practice is to help you find a place in nature that feels particularly potent to you—a spot where you can work with the spirits without being bothered by anything. If you can find the genius loci of the area as previously mentioned, all the better. As we saw in chapter 9, this will be the most potent place for any animist work. If that is not possible, take time to stop and open all your senses to your animal self. Once in this feral state, open to the Other and the nature spirits, walk with spirits, open and allow yourself to be drawn more easily to the right place of power for the work you want to do, especially if it concerns a spirit-kin animal.

Once you find the place that seems right to you, sit and hum for a time to make sure it feels right. Rely on your primal animal self to guide you in this. Open to your primal intuition, consult your instincts, and just feel into the place. This special place is crucial. If you live on a large piece of land and can find the right spot, perfect! If you live in an apartment or small house, try exploring a bit to find a healthy natural spot—a room or porch or balcony that is full of plants may work if it is imbued with the right energy. Keep in mind that you will be doing rituals that involve humming, clapping, or chanting, so be sure to choose a place where you won't be bothered by other humans.

Open your consciousness and ask yourself: Is this place full of the *wildness* of nature? Do you feel the vast interwoven fabric of nature that can lead to a deep interaction and spiritual connection with the Earth Mother? Does it offer a door that opens up to the liminal world of the nature spirits? As you sit there with your animal self and your senses open, can you sense or see the nature spirits all around you? Your intuition will help you answer these questions. Thank the spirits and the Earth Mother. With meditations and intuitive magickal work, all these forces will be woven together with help from the nature spirits, as well as from the animal spirit friend you want to contact.

When you feel that this sacred wildness has become a part of you, you can begin to call to the spirit-kin animal through the simple rituals and tools you have already mastered. Begin by opening your primal spiritual self and, arms open, let its light shine out from your heart to form a sphere of light. When you infuse your work with your will, your love, and intensive visualization, you let the spirit-kin animal know that you are seeking a deeper connection with them. This is especially true when you open up to your spirit-kin animal presence and invite it to join you.

Begin your work with simple intuitive practices already mentioned and rituals that can forge deeper connections with your spirit-kin animal. You may use your feral instincts to craft your own practices and simple rites that incorporate elements from this book and of the natural world around you—including earth, stones, plants, trees, flowers, herbs, water, animal fur, feathers, bones, and appropriate found offerings and items the spirits leave for you. The nature spirits will offer you some ideas as your bond with them grows. As always, let such spirits guide you in this. With intuition, their support, and wisdom you will be drawn more deeply into their world. Be sure to honor them with offerings, and remember to thank the Earth Mother and record your experiences in your journal.

PRACTICE
Working from Your Place of Power

You can honor nature spirits anytime or anywhere, but your feral magick will always be more effective when performed in the wild—and especially from your place of power. You can reach out and work with nature spirits and your spirit-kin animal partner when you are hiking through a wilderness area, or strolling in a forest, or walking along a beach, or climbing a mountain—anywhere you feel the urge to connect with the nature spirits all around you. This is especially true when you are trying to commune with green nature spirits like those of trees, grasses, bushes, fungi, or with water spirits like lakes, rivers, and oceans or others. And of course it is true for a variety of other kinds of spirits as well.

When you reach out to nature spirits from your place of power, you experience their energies and learn how they can be directed toward a specific purpose like self-healing. Different natural areas and primal places contain very different nature spirits and you can learn from any of them if you approach them in the right way. You do not need to perform complicated ceremonies or make elaborate offerings. Just use your intuition and bring along some simple animal-safe food items like nuts and berries, a snip of your hair, and some pure water. You can also bring a rattle or wooden rhythm sticks or any other items to help you focus and conjure.

When you have found a place in nature that feels right to you and where you can be alone, face north or east and breathe deeply to center yourself. With each breath, sway back and forth gently, and enter a light trance state. Stop, place your hands on your heart, enter a trance, then open your arms and your spirit-self light and expand its glow into a sphere around you. Feel it center and empower your core.

Then stand, go into a liminal deeper trance, and open your arms to nature and to the spirits around you by vibrating "Ahhh Haa Yahh" three times, then hum a sequence that feels right to you repeatedly as the spirits begin to manifest, often as glimmers. Close your eyes slightly and, when you sense the presence of curious nature spirits, vibrate "Pa Tan

Heya" to welcome them. With your arms out, sway and embrace all of nature and all the nature spirits. They will be happy to be acknowledged. Be open, loving, aware and listen and accept.

Pour out a bit of the water and offer a bit of your hair as a "calling card," as you open to the spirits about you with love and curiosity and joy. Pay attention to them, then hum whatever pattern comes to you from them. Let it flow and build and become clear. With will and love, commune with these delightful spirits. Listen to them and get to know them. They may be quite different from other spirits that dwell in many different places you have visited.

When your work is done, slow and soften your humming sequence or other rhythmic pattern. Bow and thank these unique spirits, and honor them with love and gratitude for reaching out. Drink some water and pour out the rest to the spirits with gratitude in your heart. Then scatter the simple offerings to them. Then center yourself and, with open arms, bring your primal spirit light back into your heart and clasp your hands over your heart center to seal it there. Touch the earth with both hands and silently thank the Earth Mother and all the wonderful new spirits you have met for giving you wisdom and joy.

As always, be sure to record your experience and anything you learned in your journal.

CHAPTER 13

DEEPENING YOUR SPIRIT-PARTNER CONNECTION

When you have achieved a connection with your spirit-kin animal partner, it's time to open communication with it. But remember—that communication has to go both ways. As humans in a human world, we have been taught that things are either real and concrete, or ephemeral. But when you walk the spirit path, you are dealing with something that is "other" than what you are used to. Spirit essences are something different—they are conscious in a way that we generally don't perceive or understand. When you open yourself up to their world—for instance, in a trance state—you open yourself up to a world in which consciousness and unconsciousness coexist and overlap.

I have been around Animists who assume that this way of living is a normal way of functioning in reality. But for most of us, it takes a little practice to feel comfortable in a world where consciousness and unconsciousness function together. This reality falls outside our limited human constructs, which are based on the programming we have received about what is real and what is not. When you reach out to spirit-kin animals and they reach out to you, it's like looking in a mirror. When you take a step toward your spirit-kin animal partner, it has already taken a step toward you—or, more accurately, toward the animal self that resonates within you.

There are two ways that you can deepen the connection between your consciousness and the consciousness of the spirit being that calls to you—through images and visions, and through vocalizations.

Images and Visions

Images and visions are gifts that are given to you by many of the spirits to enhance your connection with them. Images are actual pictures of people or animals or things that your spirit partner shows you that you can draw or paint, or in some way record for later use. Visions are more ephemeral and often transitory, and generally appeal to your intuition rather than your rational mind. Both are meant to be accepted without intellectual analysis.

Spirit-kin animals often communicate visually in your mind, offering impressions, suggestions, and symbols that can be deeply personal and very important. These images are sometimes clearer than the usual wavering images in your mind. As you'd expect, spirit-kin animal spirits do not think or communicate in the way humans do, and each interaction and communication will be as unique as your relationship is. They communicate with iconic or indexical signals but can be taught to communicate using symbols as well.

Images and visions open nonverbal, telepathic conversations between you and your spirit partner. These communications may surface first during meditation or in a trance state, but as you increase your focus and the connection between you and your spirit-kin animal grows, they will likely increase and flow more easily. The more you connect with an animal spirit, the faster it learns how to communicate with you. Because these spirits are deep and ancient beings, this makes sense. In fact, I discovered that some of the images that the wolf spirit gave to me as we bonded it turned out were actually ancient symbols.

If you become aware of confusing symbols or images, draw them in your journal and research them online later. Also, meditate on them if they are unique. Then meditate on them with your spirit-kin animal and be open to understanding what is being communicated. You'll find a practice that can help you do that at the end of this chapter. Work on visualizing and understanding the symbols, images, messages, and feelings you receive and be open to explanations. As you develop a deeper, more personal relationship, you will build bridges between you that can lead to an increasingly satisfying interaction and friendship.

Vocalizations

As you become closer to your personal spirit-kin animal, you may begin to hear it sending auditory messages. These may be feral sounds like a caw or a growl or a howl, or they may be tunes or humming patterns. When this happens, this spirit partner is offering you yet another way to communicate—another way to span the divide the separates you. Shamans have been doing this for eons. Be sure to keep notes of all of these experiences and use them to help you develop personal rituals that will resonate with your being and awareness, as well as with that of the animal spirit that seeks to work with you.

When the wolf spirit came to me, a kind of sound echoed clearly within my mind, a variety of howls. I was shocked as I distinctly heard these sounds. They immediately seemed to prompt mental and psychic shifts in my reality. Once I was able to comprehend what was going on, I began to sense the various meanings of each sound, and this ultimately allowed me to communicate and work directly with the wolf spirit. As I researched wolf sounds—including growls, rumbles, play barks, and so on—I learned to use them appropriately and our personal bond grew. Of course, I received direct images and nonverbal messages as well. But oddly, the more I learned and understood about the animalistic wolf "language," the clearer all our communication became.

Sometimes the animal vocalizations you hear in your mind point to important ways in which you can build communication with your animal-spirit partner. When your animal-spirit partner seeks to communicate in this way, be open to understanding the messages being sent—whether through psychic communications, mental impressions, animalistic sounds, visual images, or direct nonverbal feelings. Learn to sense these messages and record them in your journal so you can review them later. This will help you build upon your understanding and develop your competence.

Every relationship between the mundane and spirit world is different, and your relationship to your spirit-kin animal will be unique. Be sensitive; be open; be loving. And be patient as you work with your spirit-kin animal partner. Keep in mind that you are venturing into another world. Think of it as traveling to an unfamiliar country. Be caring and pay attention to the feral inhabitants of that mysterious land. Observe the different ways of thinking, communicating, and connecting you find there. Imagine you are an anthropologist in a strange, new Neo-Animist world, and be open to all things unusual and different.

PRACTICE

Vision Meditation

When meditating on visions you have received, it is best to do it in your special feral place—your place of power (see chapter 12). Working in this powerful place builds energy and more easily opens you to the spirit-kin animal you are contacting. Eventually, this place will become a familiar location in which you and your animal-spirit partner can meet. This process can also be used for other nature spirits. I work with tree spirits a lot.

Take some simple tools with you—a rattle, or bell, or rhythm sticks, or perhaps a flute or a simple wooden whistle. Always bring along water for drinking and to honor the spirits, and a small, natural container of offerings that are safe for all animals. It's a good idea to bring a medium-size natural blanket or cloth that you can sit on, as well as some dried herbs to scatter or burn. You can also bring amulets, images, and other items that are related to or "requested" by your spirit-kin animal partner. Carry all these items in a shoulder bag made of a natural material and dress in all-natural clothing. If you are working at night, bring a small flashlight or candle and make sure you are dressed warmly. And of course, always bring your journal.

Find (or bring) a flat stone that you can use as a spirit tablet or altar. Cleanse it of any negative influences by washing it in a solution of pure running water and salt. Hum a sequence or vibrate sounds like "Ahaa Yaa" as you do this (see chapter 7). Set up all the things you brought at your special feral spot in nature. Then sit and relax.

Open your spirit light with your hands as you have done before and expand it into a sphere. Honor the Earth Mother by placing your hands on the spirit tablet, then bow and begin to call on the spirit-kin animal or nature spirits you seek. Meditate with that spirit and ask it to grant you a vision. Your spirit partner may appear to you in a variety of visions. Much will depend on the spirit itself. When the wolf spirit comes to call on me, it is almost always in the form of a specific wolf. While that spirit is communicating, keep your mind as clear as possible. Keep your breathing calm and regular. Open your mind and quiet all the mental chaos that is there so that the spirit will have a "clear space" to enter your consciousness.

When you are in a deep, relaxed state, call to the nature spirit or spirit-kin animal with which you are connected. Open your mind, heart, and will, but in silence, not with words. You may instinctively use your rattle, or bell or clap or hum a sequence, or perhaps whistle a sequence, whatever feels right. Just let the process flow in a safe meditative space. This may take some practice. Once you feel or sense the presence of the spirit-kin animal or other spirit you seek, open your mind more fully to receiving the visions it offers. Let the vision you receive become more distinct with each deep breath. Don't "talk back" unless asked. Just be open, receptive, and silent, in the full expectation that the spirit will come.

This takes some time and effort, but the process will become easier with practice. After six years of opening to my wolf spirit and to tree spirits, the visions appear quickly and very clearly. Your spirit-kin animal partner should always look the same, with the same familiar colorations, form, and presence. Sometimes it may appear to be amused; sometimes exasperated. I have been told that this is common with such personal spirit-kin animals. It may be the same for you.

Once you and your spirit partner are deeply bonded, you may want to try this meditation at your shrine in your home. Of course, the best work is always done in the wild amid nature, but once you have established a deep connection, bringing your spirit partner into your home can help you connect to the spirit world there as well. In fact, your shrine can become a potent space where you and your animal- or nature-spirit partner can "hang out" together. This can be a powerful way to build spiritual relationships and create space for the spirit world to manifest. Whether you meditate with your spirit partner in the woods or at your home shrine, it will begin to come to you in an increasingly clearer form, and sometimes even in flashes of light, visions, or dreams. The more time you spend in these deep meditative or liminal/trance states, the more powerful your connection will become and the more your communication skills will grow.

When you are finished meditating, scatter the water and offerings about you clockwise, then open your arms and bring the light of your primal spirit back into your heart and body. And be sure to record everything in your journal—especially the images and visions! Draw, sketch, or paint the signs or symbols you saw so you can study them later. You can even focus on them before sleeping to trigger potent dream experiences. Eventually, you may even want to engrave or draw them on your spirit tablet.

PRACTICE
Basic Spirit-Kin Animal Vocalization Rite

For this practice, you will need a flat stone that you can use as an altar that is located in a secluded natural place. This can be found by accident or deliberately sought, provided that it is imbued with feral energy to support your magick. Or you can bring the spirit tablet that you use in your rituals at home with you.

On this stone, place a cup of pure water, a small rough-hewn plate or bowl for food offerings, a small container holding appropriate herbs or plants to be burned or presented, a small or medium-size drum or rattle, and some leaves, grasses, or flowers gathered from the around the stone. All these items should be simple, primitive, and primal. They work best if you find or craft them yourself. The drum or rattle should be made of a natural material and carved or decorated with a symbol that indicates the spirit-kin animal you are contacting. The plants can be arranged however you like. If you will be working at night, be sure to have a beeswax candle in a natural holder at hand. If you like, you can also place natural intoxicants or other items on the stone.

When you are ready to begin, stand before the altar stone and breathe deeply, expanding your consciousness to fill the area of nature around the ritual place. Listen in silence and look at everything expectantly. The power of wild nature will offer you a clear sign that natural forces are present—perhaps a bird's cry, a hovering butterfly, or a ray of sunlight.

Pour some of the water on the stone and, with your eyes closed, vibrate "Huua Huuuuuuu Huuuuuu" to draw the attention of all the animalistic spirits in the area. Light or crush the herb you brought (depending on if you are calling on your spirit-kin animal or all the animalistic spirits) and sprinkle it in a counterclockwise direction around the stone while vibrating "Haaaa Haaaa Haaaa" to banish all human or other negative energies.

Place your hands on the stone altar and honor its spirit, and all the spirits now gathering about the altar, as well as the Earth Mother, and vibrate "Maaaa Maaaa Maaaa." Intoxicants may be offered or utilized at this time while vibrating "uuuUuuuuuuUuuuuu." Take up the drum or rattle and begin to play with your eyes closed, seeking the right drum beat for the spirit being called. This may take time. Intone "AHhhh HaYa AHhhh HaYa AHhhh HaYa" as many times as needed.

Stand with your eyes slightly opened and out of focus, then begin swaying side to side while playing the same rhythm. Exhale while vibrating "Ahhhh Ha Ya, Ahhhh Ha Ya, Ahhhh Ha Ya" until that spirit whispers a vocalization—a low growl or howl, or the caw of a crow, or the hiss of a puma. Let your animal self intuit the sound and let it flow through you. Once you have identified it, utter the appropriate animal call, and let your conscious mind sink into a deep, dark liminal state.

If you see the right spirit-kin animal arise from this deep place in the form of the animist spirit you are calling, you are on the right track. Keep your eyes partly closed and unfocused and see that spirit rise above the altar and stare at you. As you continue to drum or rattle, begin a swaying dance, rocking and spinning about several times as you "speak and sing" with this spirit-kin animal, uttering whatever sounds that are appropriate. Maybe a low caw for a crow spirit, or a howl for a wolf spirit, or the hiss of a snake, or the growl of a bear, all depending on the animal spirit being invoked.

Let your trance state deepen with each spin or sway. Ride the rhythm and open your animal self fully to the spirit partner you are contacting. When that spirit partner begins to offer visions or "speaks" to you internally, collapse on the ground, let go of the drum or rattle, and begin to rumble, making a deep growling or purring sound deep in your chest with your mouth closed as you receive the input. Let each rumble become a longer and longer vibration as you slide into a deeper trance state and the visions or interactions with your spirit partner intensify.

When the spirit-kin animal is done and releases you, honor it as a dear friend and continue rumbling, pick up the drum or rattle, and begin to shake or beat a new rhythm of thanks and farewell. Do this intuitively, slowly, and with guidance from the departing spirit. Slowly rise and continue your deep rumbling, as a new rhythm now comes to you. Rock forward and back as you let go of the trance state. When your spirit partner is gone, vibrate "Ahuuuuu Ahuuuuuuu Ahuuuuuu" and end with the sound of the animal spirit you invoked.

As the power of the spirit-kin animal fades and you fully come back to your body, begin to walk counterclockwise about the altar while beating a new, simple, earthing rhythm and repeating "Aha Aha Aha" several times. As you do so, feel your human consciousness rise from the deep well of your inner mind as the influence of the spirit partner flies from your mind.

Take time to sit and write or draw everything about the encounter in your journal. When you are done, pour out the remaining water, food, and herbs onto the stone. Place your hands on the stone and honor the Earth Mother by vibrating "Maaa Maaa Maaa," then say whatever blessing you wish to honor the animal spirit. Gather up the items you brought and go, leaving the offerings on the stone altar.

That night, before you sleep, use your drum or rattle to recreate the rhythm the animal spirit gave you. Vibrate "Huuu Huuu Huuu" as you fall asleep, while visualizing the spirit. Of course, when you awaken, record any dreams or visions you received in your journal immediately.

PRACTICE

Establishing a Deeper Animal-Partner Communion

This simple rite can help you achieve a deeper communion with your spirit-kin animal. Keep in mind that all spirits, like you, have autonomy and agency. Forget what you read in books on ceremonial magick about "commanding spirits." We are talking about connecting with nature spirits in their own world. You cannot control these spirits, and trying to do so is a serious mistake. These are some of the oldest, deepest, most primordial beings that have ever existed, and they determine whether or not they will create loving bonds with you. So when you call on an animal spirit, do so in the same way that you would call on a good friend to request their presence or seek help—ask, but never command. I ask for help or mentoring from the wolf spirit I'm bonded with fairly often, and it has helped, guided, and set me straight a few times, when it so wills. Nature spirits have much greater wisdom than we do, and we must honor that wisdom by approaching them respectfully and offering our energy and our love when requested.

Here is a simple way to reach out to your spirit-kin animal in this manner. It's especially useful once you have a firm relationship. To perform this rite, you will need a rattle or small drum (or simply yourself), appropriate animal-safe offerings such as nuts and berries, a natural vessel of pure water, a small twig or branch of a tree you intuitively feel connects with your spirit-kin animal partner, and a small cloth of a color that connects with what feels right for you. You can make this rite as simple or as complex as you like. One way you can make it more complex is by incorporating tools like the *I Ching* or a tarot deck. As always, let the nature spirits guide you.

You can perform this rite at your spirit shrine, but feral magick always works best when performed in the wild. If possible, find a place outside or in the woods—perhaps a place of power or, better yet, the genius loci of the area. If you are working outside, bring your spirit tablet with you, or identify a flat stone that can serve as your altar.

When you are ready to begin, spend some time opening up your animal self. Then stand before your spirit tablet facing north or east. Hold up the small twig or branch with your eyes closed or partially closed and breathe deeply as you have done before to center yourself. With each breath, sway back and forth gently and enter a light trance state. Open your own glowing primal spirit and let its light shine out from your heart center. With your arms open, extend the light until it forms a sphere around you. Let your swaying motion become more like a dance and hum a sequence that comes to you.

Use the small branch to "sweep" the area as you move in a circle clockwise. Feel and see the power of the Earth Mother and all that is alive sweeping and swirling about you as a billowing green light, removing all negativity with the primal power of nature. Then raise the branch higher, extend your arms, and begin to hum a new pattern to call your spirit partner. When you are finished, plant the branch in the earth behind the tablet and call out to your spirit-kin animal with its own cry—a caw, a howl, a hiss; whatever is appropriate.

Pour a bit of the water over the branch and place some of your offerings around it as you sway or dance. Humming the same pattern, pick up the rattle or drum and use it to gently call to the spirit with a rhythm that feels right to you.

Sit with your eyes almost closed and a bit out of focus until you feel the spirit's presence. Be silent, but gently shake your rattle to open the connection between you. After the spirit has acknowledged you, silently ask it for the help or wisdom or guidance you need. Continue this communion for as long as you feel necessary. Be confident that the help will come.

When the work is done, shift your humming and rattling into another different calm rhythmic pattern, one that is quieter and slower and feels right. Bow and thank your spirit-kin animal partner, and honor it with love. Drink some water and pour out the rest over the small branch. Scatter the rest of the offerings in a clockwise circle and bid the spirit farewell with a final humming, a song, or some other impromptu utterance.

When you sense that the spirit is gone, pick up the branch and spin around counterclockwise, sweeping the circle with it. Make the cry of your spirit-kin animal three times to send all the energies flying. Center yourself and pull all the light of your primal spirit back into your heart, and seal it there by clasping your hands over your heart center. Touch the earth with both hands and thank the Earth Mother by vibrating "Maaaa." Then sit in silence for a time.

As always, be sure to record the experience and any answers you receive in your journal.

CHAPTER 14

BONDING AND TRANCE STATES

The world is full of life and wonder. Once you have opened up to the idea that all things are alive and that the world is full of a variety of nature spirits, you can begin to open yourself up to deep connections with the spirit-kin animal that has called to you and which you seek. When you truly accept that the world of nature spirits is absolutely real—as you did when you were a child— their world will welcome and open to you and they will often guide, mentor, teach, and protect you.

When you were a child, mystical creatures and magickal beings seemed completely natural. All things were wondrous and you could speak to trees and birds and animals. They probably "spoke" to you. But that was before you were told by adults that the world was not the magickal place you thought it was. What a let-down. But let me share a secret with you: You were right and they were wrong!

In many ways, the purpose of this book is to encourage you to become that child again and embrace the spirits and the joy of nature that animated your world as a child. By accessing nature, you can once again be as open, as joyful, and as full of wonder as you were then. I know this is true because I have visited many people who live this way. The tribal Mien people in the mountains of Thailand see the world in this way, as do the Nani Doro people of Siberia, and the millions of Japanese who see the world as a wondrous miraculous place full of kami: tree spirits, river spirits, and animal spirits like kitsune, and more. The

Japanese refer to the Other, the world of nature spirits, as "the floating world" and this is as good a term as any.

If this all feels right to you, try doing this simple meditation outside in nature in a place where you won't be disturbed. Find a quiet, green place that feels right to you, then relax and breathe in the rich air. Take time to remember your childhood and the many magickal things that delighted you when you were young. Close your eyes and remember the child that you were. In your mind, relive the interactions you had with nature. Open your mind to a time when all was wonder and joy. Revisit your imaginary playmates and commune with the trees and animals that delighted you then. Try to remember the animals that appeared in visions or dreams or other nature spirits you saw or felt. Recall the ones that played with you in fields or woods, and maybe in your daydreams. Let your mind wander and remember those days. Now think how nice it would be if you could reenter that world. You are closer than you realize.

Here are two practices can help you do just that.

PRACTICE

Recapturing Spirits of Childhood

For this practice, you will need a calm and relaxing bedroom, and an image or simple sketch of an animal partner or other spirit "imaginary friend" you loved and played with as a child. Meditate in liminal space for a time on the childhood image—it may actually have been something interesting, not just a fantasy, otherwise why would it leave such an impression? Finish meditating and place the sketch or image next to your bed where you can see it. Keep your journal or a notepad handy so you can record your experience.

Lie on your back on the bed and breathe slowly, relaxing with every breath. Hold a very clear image or memory of the special being you have chosen. Do your best to hold that image in your mind. Remember how wild and feral a child you were. You likely pretended to shapeshift into wild animals—I know I did! Hold that memory and remember what it felt like.

With each exhalation, reach out mentally to that special animal partner, that imaginary friend, that tree spirit or another nature being you remember. You may or may not believe it was real. But don't worry about that. Just hold the image in your mind as best you can and fall asleep gently.

If something unusual or startling happens as you are in a liminal state just before you fall asleep, sit up and write or draw what you heard or saw. If not, just fall asleep while focusing intently on the image you've been holding in your mind.

When you awaken, immediately write down any dreams or visions you had before they fade. Did you have a dream in which this spirit being showed up? If so, you had an exciting dream! Write down all the unusual experiences you had as a child that you may have forgotten, but that are now emerging from your deep consciousness. If nothing eventful occurs, try remembering more of your earliest childhood; then try this practice again.

I have had great success with this exercise. When I first did this practice, I remembered that, when I was five and my brother was three or four, we saw a small green elf spirit. It came as a bit of a shock, but we both saw it. Children see the real reality around them.

PRACTICE

Passing through the Gateway of the Spirits

This more focused practice can yield amazing results when you continue to work with your spirit-kin animal partner, though it can be used for any nature spirit you are working with. It is best done while you are awake in a place in wild nature that you have always felt was magickal—perhaps a place where gentle spirits dwell. Sit in this special magickal place and breathe deeply. Open your mind and remember how wonderful this spot was and is to you. Breathe deeply all the scents. Accept that this place is really magickal, an intersection between the hidden magickal world of nature and the mundane world of human reality. Accept it as a secret gateway to the spirit world of childhood where spirits and fairies dwell. Relax and as your trance deepens you pass through this secret gateway into the Otherworld. You begin to see a brighter, more alive world—a vibrant place that you have always known was real, a special place you can remember.

Once you are comfortable, relax your whole body and, without thinking deeply, open your mind to this really magickal place. Let your eyes drift out of focus and open to the energies that suddenly flow through the trees and earth and sky as you breathe deeply and open up. Soon you become aware of the many different shades of vibrant green that color the forest. You hear so many more sounds than you heard before. You smell the suddenly intoxicating scents of flowers, the wind, the grasses, tree sap, and the deep rich earth.

Now, get up and explore this new world. Open your five senses as you learned before. Touch the bark of a tree that now seems so amazing. Hear the birds as they talk to each other and realize that you can understand them at times. Drink in the taste of the air, the trees, the moisture around you. Lie in the grass or lean against a large tree. Then close your eyes, and breathe deeply and slowly until you are completely calm and open to the green.

Place your hands on your chest and "see" the brilliant light of your primal spirit glowing. Open your arms and see it expanding into a sphere that surrounds you. Then silently ask to connect with a special creature that you knew as a child long ago—a being or spirit who spoke with you. See its image clearly in your mind's eye. Perhaps it was an animal-spirit partner you met long ago, or perhaps it was another spirit, such as a tree spirit or river spirit.

Slowly open your eyes and look carefully around you. Can you see that spirit in front of you? If not, close your eyes and try to see it in your mind's eye. When it faintly appears, slightly open your eyes; can you see it in front of you now? It may be just a glimmer or a shadowy image, or you may simply sense a presence. Open your mind and your heart to this spirit and sense the reality of the experience—the world that we have banished from our materialistic existence has come alive. Is this real or imagination? When images become clear and real, you will know. Reach out, connect as you can. Hold that.

When you are ready to leave, open your arms and see the light of the forest embrace you. Pull that light back into your heart and seal it there by clasping your hands over your chest.

Finally, place your hands on the earth and bow, silently thanking the Earth Mother, the beautiful green nature about you, and all the animal and nature spirits. Then stand and go. As always be sure to record your experience in your journal. The more you do this simple exercise, the closer you become to the Otherworld of the nature spirits.

PRACTICE

Mentoring a Spirit-Kin Animal Bonding

This ritual relies on a light trance state to help you call to and bond with your spirit-kin animal mentor. Like the last practice, it can be done in your special primal place in nature or in any wilderness. Identify a flat stone in the area to use as a spirit tablet. Bring along any ritual tools you feel appropriate and place them on or around the altar stone.

To perform this simple ritual, you will need a container of pure water, a natural bowl for food offerings (such as seeds or berries), appropriate dried herbs (like rosemary), a sacred rattle or other rhythm tool, and three leaves taken with permission and thanks from potent trees. If you wish, you can also bring a token or icon of your spirit-kin animal partner and natural intoxicants.

Stand before the altar stone and breathe deeply. Relax completely and begin to expand your consciousness of the nature around you. Touch the glowing light of your primal spirit at your heart and extend it into a sphere of light that fills the area around you. Close your eyes slightly and let them go a bit out of focus, and breathe deeply as you enter a light trance state. Rock or sway as you like. Listen, feel, and experience the power and life of this beautiful natural world. Sense and hear and smell everything in silence, expectantly.

When you hear a woodland sound or feel a gentle brush from a nature spirit, begin to whistle a simple sequence that comes to you and call to the living spirits. Let your instinct guide you in this. Repeat the sequence for a time and feel the tones, which you may vary, opening the Otherworld further and calling to the spirits as you slide deeper into a trance state. The spirits of the forest, the green soul of wild nature, will offer a sign. It may be the cry of a bird, or a gust of breeze, or the growl of a wild animal, or just a sudden feeling that many natural forces are gathering and spirits are gently moving you into the Other.

When it feels right, spill some water on the earth and, with your eyes closed, vibrate "Ahaa Yah." Then shake your rattle or other tool and, as things shift, vibrate "Huu Huuuuuuu Huuuuuu" to draw the attention of all the nature spirits in this area to you. Crush the herbs you brought and scatter them clockwise in a circle, offering them to the nature spirits. As you inhale the scent of the herbs, open your mind to the spirits, and especially to your spirit-kin animal, as you begin a rhythmic chant that honors them and expresses joy—"Haaaa Haaaa." As you do so, all your mundane human energies and other negative vibrations will be banished.

Place your hands on the stone altar and honor your spirit-kin animal partner as well as all the nature spirits now gathered around the altar. Then honor the Earth Mother by vibrating "Maaaa Haaa, Maaaa Haaa, Maaaa Haaa." Pour out some pure water on the edge of the stone tablet, then clasp your hands and vibrate "Pa Tan He Ya" three times. Using a rattle or your hands, begin a rhythm that comes to you directly from your spirit-kin animal. With your eyes closed, open to all the spirits and bring them all together dancing about you and your spirit-kin partner. Call forth your animal self, your deep primal being, by rocking and vibrating and uttering primal sounds received from your spirit-kin animal. Then shift to a rhythmic chant of "Ahhhh Ha, Ahhhh Ha, Ahhhh Ha," repeating it as many times as feels right. Don't worry if this chant changes.

You will feel and likely perceive your spirit-kin animal clearly in your inner mind or before you. It may hover above or before you. You will feel its presence intensely, as the chants and the rhythms, as well as the joy of all the spirits, have helped clarify it. You will feel joy as this bond deepens and you open to the experience.

Begin swaying side to side and open your eyes slightly. On the tool of your choice, begin to play a new rhythm indicating "bonding together" and sing the chant "Ahhhh Ya, Ahhhh Ya, Ahhhh Ya" until your spirit-kin animal whispers a different chant to you—perhaps a low growl, or a howl, or the caw of a crow, or the hiss of a snake. Let your spirit-kin animal channel the right sound through you.

Once you have it, keep rocking side to side, and set a new rhythm, becoming more and more feral as your animal self settles into a deeper feral trance with your spirit-kin animal. As you do so, begin to utter the wild animalistic calls of your spirit-kin animal as you release your conscious mind and sink deeper into the trance and become one with your primal feral being. Feel the collective joy of all the nature spirits around you as you are embraced by wild nature.

As the trance deepens with you both bonding together, feel the spirit-kin animal filling your being with a tingling power as you continue using your rattle or clapping. Begin to rock forward and back, exhaling as you move forward and inhaling as you move back. Rumble as you inhale to deepen your bond.

As your animal self and your spirit-kin partner's consciousness become entwined, your animalistic mind is flooded with new thoughts and feelings, images and energy that may be alien to you but are comprehensible to your animal self. From within your animal self, a new humming sequence will fill you and erupt from you. Begin to dance with your spirit-kin animal partner in a way that feels right to you, happily swaying and rocking with joy. Hum or sing as feels right as your animal self speaks.

Together with your spirit-kin animal partner, utter cries and chants and whistles and humming—whatever comes as the spirit-kin animal flows through you and with you. Let a deeper trance state take you as you move and spin and sway. Ride the rhythm as one, and open fully to this moment. Let it flow.

When the ecstasy begins to fade, slow your motions and sit or even lie on the ground. Breathe deeply and be silent and completely open as your spirit-kin animal partner shows you visions, important symbols, or places. Listen as it whispers special sounds, words, or secrets. Let the earth comfort you. Let go of everything. Breathe in deeply as the Earth Mother steadies and fills you. Be one with your animal spirit for a time. Begin to rumble deep in your chest to calm and center yourself. Soon each rumble becomes longer, softer, and lower as your trance state and the visions or interactions with the spirit soften and begin to fade. Your union gently dissolves, but the connection between you doesn't.

Soon, your spirit-kin animal will gently separate from you and hover nearby as you both silently honor each other and let go. As it leaves you, continue the soft, low rumbling as you slowly come back from the trance, with the earth gently pulling you and supporting you. With your rhythm tool, begin a slow three-beat pattern with the last beat harder as you sway. Release your animal self and sink back down into your deep inner shadow self as your human mind gently rises.

Sitting or standing, breathe deeply and gently vibrate "Ah Ha," then open your arms wide to embrace the sphere of light around you. Pull the light back into your heart and body, and seal it there by placing your hands over your heart center. Stand facing the altar with your arms raised and vibrate "Huuuuu Huuuuuuu Huuuu" as you visualize your animal self quieting and the realm of the nature spirits fading.

Scatter the rest of the herbs you brought in a counterclockwise circle and inhale their scent deeply to bring you back into your body. Begin a "farewell" rhythm that feels right to you, stomping your feet to it as you leave the trance state and come completely back into your body. To close the ritual, vibrate "Ahuuuuu Ahuuuuuuu Ahuuuuuu" in high to low tones. As the world of the nature spirits fades, walk about the altar sprinkling the food offerings and water you brought. Honor your partner spirit-kin animal as feels right to you.

Place your hands on the spirit tablet, then bow and honor the Earth Mother by vibrating "Maaa Maaa Maaa." Let any excess energies flow to her. Then pack away your things and pour any remaining water on the spirit tablet. You can leave any remaining food offerings, provided they are animal-safe. Be sure to record everything about the encounter in your journal.

That night, as you fall asleep, remember the many communicated blessings your spirit-kin animal gave you, while visualizing your animal self. Of course, when you awaken, write down any dreams or visions you have in your journal immediately.

CHAPTER 15

SHAPESHIFTING

Shapeshifting is not always what it sounds like. The practice of feral shamanic shapeshifting involves going into a very deep trance state so that you have access to the Other. Traditional animalistic shamanic shapeshifting can involve physical transmutation, but usually this form of shapeshifting is magickal and deep-trance spiritual, and not often physical. If you have been using the practices given in previous chapters, you have been doing this already in some ways. When you enter a light trance state to unleash your feral animal self, you are initiating a kind of feral shapeshifting. This kind of gentle shifting can help forge more powerful relationships with nature spirits or even a spirit-kin animal that has bonded with you. Taking this trance work to shapeshift with the spirit-kin animal you are deeply bonded with opens into a much deeper union, a joint feral shapeshifting, and, as one, you become something very different and more powerful, though how deep you want to go is up to you.

Done correctly, a conjoined trance-shapeshift state calls for a dance or interaction with animal spirits and the animal self. If done well and deeply, this shifting state helps you merge with your spirit-kin animal. This sort of shapeshifting is sometimes referred to as a kind of spirit possession, but not in a horror movie kind of way. This is a shamanic, intentional form of possession. Various forms of this have been used in many cultures by shamans, sorcerers, and others for eons. This kind of shapeshifting can be applied to expand the deep intuitive and ongoing connection between you and your spirit-kin animal partner, enabling you to mesh with one another and so communicate intuitively and psychically. In a sense, your consciousness can actually *connect* with the consciousness of your spirit-kin animal. Thus it allows you to more deeply bond with each other, so you may be linked whenever you wish it, even when you are not in a ritual trance consciousness. You will gain a deeper interconnectivity with one another, and be able to understand and communicate more intuitively and psychically.

This kind of joint-spirit-shapeshifting is one I have been using for many years to allow my feral animal self to arise and thus let the wolf spirit bond with me and help me fully shift to "were" mode. When this happens, the spirit helps me quiet my upper cortex, as my primal human-self emerges more fully. This has helped me on many physical, spiritual, and emotional levels, and has solidified my relationship with my wolf spirit partner, especially during full moons. This merging of a wolf animal spirit with my feral self results in a cooperative mentoring or gentle co-possession. This is one way I believe shamans work and bond with their spirit-kin animals and nature spirits. Think of it as an equation: wolf spirit kin + my feral animal self = werewolf, or "human-wolf." This is not myth; it is what some shamans do when working with their animal spirits. While you are not a shaman—nor am I—you can use this technique to help you with your Neo-Animist work.

Such beneficial shapeshifting lets you build up a new or stronger relationship with your spirit-kin animal that can have ongoing benefits. It makes stepping into the Other spirit world easier and opens up ongoing communication between you. It also brings a wider awareness and an ability to feel and interact with all kinds of nature spirits. In fact, "shapeshifting" and bonding like this can help you work more easily with any kind of interested nature spirit as well as your spirit-kin animal.

The next practice will introduce you to further techniques of shapeshifting. The goal is to more intensely unleash your primal feral animal self and bond with your spirit-kin animal, *animal to animal*. Before doing this more intense practice, spend time in the woods, connecting deeply with and honoring Gaia, the Earth Mother and source of all life. Spend time accessing your animal self in the woods and at home, not speaking and being animalistic and feral. Unleashing your feral animal self helps to place you into a deep communion with Mother Nature, and this is a very powerful union on many levels, as you'll see.

In the following tandem shapeshifting practice, you move from communion with nature to direct communion with your spirit-kin animal by reaching out to and connecting with the power and presence of a spirit with which you are already connected. This is a very personal kind of shapeshifting that requires dedication from both you and your spirit-kin animal. You *both* need to decide how serious and deep this powerful shapeshifting practice will be. It is, in a way, very personal. This kind of "tandem shapeshifting" should be done in the woods away from all people, if at all possible. Such shifting work demands focus, will, commitment, and energy, as well as familiarity with intermediate trance states, intense visualization, a deep and loving bond with the spirit-kin animal, and a strong will. Note that many shamans and others utilize entheogens when doing such work. However, this is up to you.

Before you begin, stop talking, listening, and thinking in your human language for a day or more. Be internally, externally, and mentally *silent in animal-self mode*. Work on promoting liminal and trance states through simple and traditional body motions, such as rocking, swaying, shaking, leaping, and other movements and gestures that come naturally to you. Spend time in real wilderness and there unleash and enjoy the experience as your animal self within the beauty and power you find there. Leave your human and ego self. Silence it. Be a feral animal.

Practice rumbling while in a light feral trance. Sway or rock and vibrate. Finally, practice unleashing your feral animal self alone in the woods. Practice focusing on the gut chakra "fire center" and use intuitive sounds, motions, or gestures, and visualization. Your spirit-kin animal will acknowledge and welcome this power, as it will be drawn to this positive force. Practice doing rituals in the woods with little or no clothes or with loose, relaxed clothing.

Here are some other things you can practice to prepare yourself for this ritual:

- Swaying side to side, casting off all thoughts and energies of the human world.
- Inhaling deeply through your nose and exhaling slowly through your mouth in sync with a forward-and-back rocking motion.
- Let free-flowing intuitive dancing and movements erupt from you as your feral animal self takes over and moves and enjoys your being.
- Seeing the world around you shift and the Other opening as you expand into nature, below and about you and above you, and seeing the energy ripple outward as you enter the world of the spirits.
- Seeing energies swirl about you and blend together as you join with your spirit-kin animal.
- As things get weird, and they will, focusing on the spirit tablet or altar as the center of the liminal sphere.
- Deepening your trance by vibrating "Ah" as you exhale and "Ha" as you inhale.
- Sensing and seeing the spirits of nature as they move and swirl about you as the spirit world unfolds.

Note that any part of this rite can be changed as the spirit-kin animal and you jointly decide. As you both review and contemplate this process, feel free to add things to the rite as you both will!

When You Are Ready to Begin This Rite

Set up your spirit tablet with your chosen items as you have done for previous practices. If you are using a candle, light it and light the herb or herbs you are using as well. Put on any talisman or other feral magick items you desire to wear.

I wear a single, very old wolf tooth that was not obtained as the result of a killing. I had a feral friend who wore shed snakeskin from her boa, and my animistic crow-spirit friend always keeps crow and raven feathers in his hair when he does animal-self shifting work. If you are using animal parts as part of the ritual, make sure they are obtained in a humane, respectful way, and not as the result of violence against an animal. Be open to what your spirit-kin animal partner suggests.

Be open, be creative, be feral. *Make this working yours.* Contemplate the previous rites offered in this book to practice and plan for this ritual.

SHIFTING PRACTICE
Becoming Your Feral Self

The items used in this ritual are basically similar to the tools you have been using. As previously stated, as you contemplate this with input from your spirit-kin animal partner, you may change, add, or decide to use any number of things.

The most common ritual items would be:

+ Your stone spirit tablet

+ A rhythmic tool such as a rattle or a drum

+ Dried or fresh herbs that are right for your shifting. Some examples include rosemary, sage, or cedar bark.

+ Other collected natural items.

+ A natural candle, or even a small, safe fire if you wish for light.

+ Offerings you and your spirit-kin animal partner like.

As you prepare, remember to be open to changing and adding things that your spirit-kin animal and your animal self seek to accomplish. Your spirit-kin animal may give clear suggestions about various aspects of the rite, which your animal self would be wise to follow. Keep in mind that

I have done this rite only with a wolf spirit, so I may be a bit biased. I do not know what the experience of doing this with a bear or crow spirit would be, but it will be fun, wild, and well if you are of one mind!

Face the spirit stone tablet and begin breathing rhythmically, making long, calm, vibrating sounds—"Ah" as you exhale, "Ha" as you inhale. As you do so, enter a liminal space and "see" and feel the reality of the spirit world as it opens around you. Touch your heart with both hands as your spirit glows in your chest with brilliant light. See it grow brighter as you continue your rhythmic breathing. Open your arms wide and see the brilliant light of your spirit expand into a beautiful sphere that surrounds you. Vibrate "Aha" as one sound and place your hands together as all becomes still and you feel centered.

Slowly unleash your animal self while swaying from side to side. Visualize then make your primal self rise. Let your mind and ego become still, calm, and silent. See your human consciousness sink into the darkness deep within, sinking lower with every deep breath. With every inhalation, see and feel your wild feral animal self rise and fill your body with feral glee! Your thinking will stop; your senses will open, and you will be suddenly immersed in the Other spirit world. The Otherworld is all around you and you become conscious of the nature spirits gathering all around you!

Begin rumbling with every exhalation. As your breathing and rumbling slow, you become fully aware of your animal self—fully awake in nature, like every other animal.

Face the stone spirit tablet and begin to rock forward and back, vibrating a deep "Ahhh" as you inhale and a deep "Yaaa" as you exhale. Sink into a purely feral consciousness as you glow from the warmth arising from the fire center in your lower belly and filling you. See and feel your animal self opening more as you sense and even see the nature spirits gathering around you.

Slow your rocking and become still. Open your hands and focus your mind toward the spirit tablet. Pour some water around the stone and softly give voice to the cry of your animal spirit as it joins with you in this. The soft animalistic sound rises and expands as your spirit-kin animal partner comes closer.

As the sound echoes through the woods, half close your eyes and open your arms as you feel and "see" the shimmer of your spirit as it approaches. With a vibrating call of "Ahh Yaaa," open your heart with love and will, and sense the shimmer of your partner's presence. As it gets closer, begin to hum a repetitive sequence—perhaps one your spirit-kin animal conveys to you as its energy touches you and hovers close to your heart. Sense its presence as the light of your spirit-kin animal and your spirit join and become one. Take time to commune with one another and feel the mental and physical bond fill you. It helps to hum in sequences you both feel.

Take time to commune with each other and continue humming while also breathing slowly and deeply as the mental and physical bonding fills you.

Rock together back and forth and then quietly vibrate "Huuuuu" over and over as your consciousness merges into a purely feral animal consciousness. Do this until you feel you are one. Then reach down and touch the stone tablet to honor the Earth Mother. Dig your claws deep into the earth and repeatedly vibrate "Aha Maaaaa" as your merged consciousness extends deep into the earth—all the way to the core, until your fire touches her fire, and you feel her power as it rises and fills you both. You may even see her eyes.

Slowly, still vibrating "Aha Maaa" deep in your chest, raise your arms to the side and embrace the trees and plants and flowers, and the green spirit of all life around you. You hear a laugh on the wind as you slowly and repeatedly vibrate "Haaaa," until you and your spirit partner together extend your glowing light out into the wildness and touch all the assembled spirits. Together, you both inhale and the green energy fills you both like pure water.

Slowly raise your arms to the sky and call to its endless power. Feel the life of the infinite cosmos above you and extend your merged consciousness upward while deeply vibrating "Laaaa." Feel the infinite immensity of the cosmos gently fill you both as you inhale. Feel the spirit of the cosmos gently fall upon you like a soft rain. Know that you and the cosmos have become one in consciousness.

As you sit and allow this all to settle, you know that the veil has parted and that everything around you is alive and vibrating. Everything is humming. See it. Hear it. Smell it. Taste it. Touch it. Open to it. You and your spirit-kin animal partner begin humming with it. As you do, your trance state deepens.

After a time, bring your hands together at your heart and sense that the light of both you and your spirit partner glows brightly as you become the center of all. Begin to shake your rattle or tap your drum and sway as all the energies of nature you have summoned fill you. Stand and let the rhythm guide you as you and your spirit partner dance slowly and spin. A great illumination fills you and all becomes light.

As you both let the rhythm fall silent, you come back into your conjoined animal selves together, gently swaying and breathing as you did before. When all stops, center yourself. Deeply and loudly exhale "Ahhhhhh Haaaaaa" three times and spin slowly about the glowing space you have manifested. Stop in the center, and sit in silence. Just listen and receive. As the visions and intense input fade, embrace the presence of your spirit-kin animal partner as it embraces you. Be still and honor each other as you mind-meld into your union.

Then, after a time, begin and repeat a new humming sequence that emerges from this moment *from you both*. As you do so, begin to sway side to side as you slowly let your animal self slide back down into its deep unconscious lair as your somewhat bewildered "normal human self" fills your mind and awakens your "normal" consciousness. Breathe deeply and stay silent as the fiery energy of your animal self slowly fades and merges with your inner primal feral being.

As this happens, your spirit-kin animal partner will begin to gently separate from your intense bond. Together, you begin to rock softly and utter the spirit-kin animal's natural cry as a gentle feral song that acknowledges the separation, even as it affirms the bond.

(For me, this is often a slow howl. For you...?)

Then, with both hands, reach up to the heavens and vibrate "Laaaaa" to honor the infinite starry expanse and the living cosmos. Reach your hands outward, embracing the living green trees and all the plants and rustling animals with a gentle "Haaaaaaaa." Honor them and offer gratitude and love. Then kneel and reach down to the Earth Mother and offer gratitude and love to the Great Mother of all. With every exhalation, the excess energy from this rite flows into her. With every inhalation, her green healing energy fills you. Close your eyes, see her eyes, and vibrate "Maaaaa."

Scatter any remaining offerings around the area. Drink some water and pour the rest out onto the earth. Stand still for a moment, and just feel and accept. Then reach out and gather all the light around you and pull it and all the other power you've gained into your heart, your spirit, and your body. Honor, commune with, and let go of your spirit partner as it does the same and slowly fades—for now.

Leave in silence and remain silent for a time when you return home. When you are ready, record everything you remember, sense, and feel about the experience in your journal. Write it. Draw it. Ruminate on it. Let the experience flow onto the pages. And know that your animal-spirit partner and you are now truly one.

Be well and be wild.

CHAPTER 16

INTUITIVE FERAL SPELLCRAFT

Everything about feral magick and Neo-Animism is about nature. Everything used for working this kind of magick has to be natural and should be gently and respectfully collected within the wilderness—for obvious reasons. In fact, there's no reason to use anything other than what nature provides when working feral magick. The spirits detest anything toxic, poisonous, abused, or anything that sickens or destroys. The key to feral spellcraft—and to our survival as a species—is a healthy wild environment. The Earth Mother has given us the elements of water and air and earth and fire, as well as the living spiritual energy of all living creatures and the spirits. With all such natural things we work our primal magickal craft, the root of feral magick.

In many ways, modern magick and occultism have removed themselves from the ancient primal natural origin of all magick, which was based on nature, the living world, the animals, and the spirits. The literal reality of the occult (hidden magick) which we were born into is a cognition-based set of abstract concepts. These are often grounded in human-centered monotheism and various religious scriptures. It is useful in some regards but, as I get older, I have come back around to my earliest feral childhood inclinations that first led me into the obvious truth that nature is and has always been the core reality behind all true magick. Most of us humans have significantly removed ourselves from what is real and have found ourselves immersed in the modern toxic chaos of our crumbling civilization. But I believe it is time to wake up to the more ancient truths that still persist in tribal and shamanic cultures. When we believe that we have souls, and animals and other living beings do not, we hasten the destruction of our environment and possibly ourselves as we poison our environment and the spirits. Yet Gaia and the spirits of nature still abide, and there is a feral wave rising among many who seek to return to the primal reality of natural magick, where our spiritual awakening awaits.

The ancient prehistoric cave paintings hold some answers to all of this if you look hard enough. The living nature spirits, the powerful spirit-kin animals, nature spirits, and the work of shamans and shapeshifters all stand ready to unveil the practices of feral magick to us. It is our job to enter the hidden wellspring of the natural world where the truths of magick lie. Nature offers us everything we need to shift, to change, to heal, to help, and to understand what we call magick. The treasures and powers that we think of as abstract have always been hidden in plain sight in the world of nature. The practices in this chapter can help you enter that world.

The spellcraft I offer here is likely a very different way of doing magickal rituals from what you will find in almost every other book on occult practices: You really don't need to be told what to do if you are working directly with the spirits of nature. All is alive and conscious in the natural world! If you enter that world as the intuitive feral being you really are—with an open and loving heart, and with respect for all natural beings—the powers and spirits of nature will accept you and support you in your work. You may be gently guided by your spirit-kin animal partner. Or you may feel moved to merge with the spirit of a particularly vibrant tree. Or a spirit may offer a leaf, a twig, or a special stone, or perhaps some sap to bring to someone who needs its energy. Be guided by your intuitive animal self and by the natural spirits who connect with you.

This is how feral magick works. The less you use frenetic thinking, the more you quiet your ego, and the more you can be open to being guided by your feral consciousness, the more help the spirits will offer and the more they will support your work—especially your spirit-kin animal partner! Your ego can't help you in this, but your primal feral animal self can bond and work with the spirits of nature, as you will be one with them!

PRACTICE
Preparing to Perform Feral Magick

In ancient times, spells and magickal practices were guided by ancient practices, deep natural knowledge, and wise instinct, without a set plan or a script. This connects with such feral practices and is intended to show you that, with a little preparation, intuition, focus, and some wisdom, you can embrace the wildness by using the ancient wisdom, help from the spirits, and your feral instincts. If your spirit-kin animal partner (or another nature spirit) agrees to come aid you on this trek, you will be more successful in every way. Just be sure to commune with your spirit-kin animal partner before you enter the wildness and honor its decision to be involved in this spellcraft and how.

As always, dress in warm comfortable clothing. Bring along some natural food items, some water, and any of the tools you have been using in other practices. You can also bring your journal and some pencils, a natural cloth or a small blanket to sit on, and any other natural items, amulets, or symbols that may help you focus and manifest your spells. Let your intuition guide you.

Small natural vessels or shells, as well as a small knife made of natural materials, may come in handy. If you will be working after dark, bring beeswax candles and matches (no plastic lighters). I also recommend that you wear appropriate shoes and bring along extra socks and handkerchiefs. Just make sure that you leave a little extra room in your rucksack so you can bring back any items offered to you by the nature spirits. As always, give thanks for and honor these gifts.

As you enter the wilderness, walk with an open mind and heart and a receptive consciousness. Use rhythmic breathing. Hum a special sequence to alert the spirits that you come as a friend who is open to their energies. Let go of your human world and let your animal self rise as you step into the natural wonders that are all about you. As you sink into your feral being, the nature spirits of the liminal world will accept you and will make that known to you.

Open all your senses and drink in all the sensations that nature and the spirits offer. Hum or whistle or shake your rattle, meditate, and breathe deeply to help you achieve a light trance state as you enter the heart of the wilderness. With every step you take, move farther along the intuitive, shifting paths of this green world and let the spirits guide and help you.

When you are in a deep liminal state, if possible, find the genius loci of the place or at least a place of power in whatever way your instincts tell you is appropriate. Sit and hum, or chant or create rhythms, or just meditate with this potent being or at the power spot that calls to you. If the place of power you have chosen "accepts" your will to do your magickal work within it, then set up your stone spirit tablet and arrange your tools and all other items you brought in a way that feels right to you.

When centered, sit, sway, hum, and maybe create rhythms as you deepen your connection with this potent place or spirit. Become one with it and offer to be fully present to all the nature spirits around you. Remain still and focused, without thinking about what needs to be done. Your goal is to let your primal intuitive powers work with the natural energies of the place to establish a connection with the nature spirits. *Just follow your will, your magickal focus, your instincts, and your creativity.*

Once you feel settled and right with this place and its spirits, place your hands on your heart, conjure your bright spirit self, and cup its light in your hands. Then open your arms and spread the light as a sphere around your place. The spirits will become interested and active and will come and go as you offer love to them. Now, relax and meditate deeply on your goal.

You may suddenly receive visions, or feel the flow of the energies of nature about you. Take out your journal and write or draw all these things as they flow through you. Remember that your spirit-kin animal or nature-spirit partners can help you all the time. Doing feral magick spellcraft in a potent place, be it a crossroads or special rock or with a genius loci, will add power to such work. Keep in mind that the deeper you can slide into your feral self, the more intuitive everything you do will be. Let your eyes close, breathe deeply as you have done in previous practices, and silently open your primal spirit light, expanding it into a sphere that surrounds you. Then open yourself completely to the nature spirits of the place using rhythms, whistles, or humming; you know what to do. If your spirit-kin animal has agreed to accompany you, repeat its particular animalistic cries, such as a caw, a hiss, or a howl, as your spirit-kin animal guides.

When all the energies and spirits are whirling and flowing, honor all the nature spirits by bowing to them with a song or humming or rhythm. Honor them with a dance or by just swaying in loving silence. Use your intuition, tools, feelings, power! Silently request that you be allowed to perform magick that draws on the forces emanating from this place for an important purpose and visualize it. Pour some pure water all around you clockwise and place some spirit offerings on and around the spirit tablet.

When you are clearly accepted in this work, profusely thank the spirits. Then sit on your cloth or blanket, relax, and prepare to do your magick.

PRACTICE

Performing Feral Magick

Once you have prepared yourself to perform feral magick, focus on the goal of this magick with your spirit-kin animal partner and with the other nature spirits who have joined you. Even if you began this work with a specific purpose, the goal may shift now that you are immersed in the energies of your place of power. If you find that this becomes true, then let shift the spell work you originally intended, relax, and open to a slightly new goal. That's how feral magick works. When you are in a feral, unthinking state, your consciousness may shift, and unexpected options may open. Suddenly what seemed important before may just fade away as the deep experience of merging with the energies of nature offers new possibilities. Just let things happen as they will, as they should, and as they need to. This is the essence of animistic feral spellcraft!

Take time to reevaluate the kind of magick you want to manifest. Be open to new feelings and ideas that flow in and around you. Do you really need money? Does a good friend need to be healed or helped in some way? Are you seeking love or friendship? Open to what feels right to you now, in the different world and space you are in. How should it be accomplished? Let your intuition and the spirits guide you. Listen! Sit and hum for a time until you find the appropriate path and goal as you listen to your spirit-kin animal partner and the other nature spirits around you. The spirits will give you a clearer understanding of what it is you need to do and why; they'll reveal the right flow.

When all flows together, face the direction that is indicated and that fits best with your intent. In the natural world, north is the primary direction for earthing things, while east is the direction where the sun rises, indicating new life, but so what? Use your instincts! Let the spirits show you. Don't think. Intuit! *Spend time opening your primal animal self to the spirits around you and let them guide you.*

Place your hands on the earth and open yourself up to the Earth Mother for guidance and power with a growl of "Maaaa!" See yourself

glowing with the light of your primal spirit. Listen and be open to specific guidance from your spirit-kin animal. Then do whatever your primal feral self indicates! Hum a special spell-tune; create rhythmic beats as the world vibrates; burn some herbs; gather stones and leaves and other items the spirits offer to you. Draw symbols in the dirt or lay them out with sticks or stones. Let it all flow and merge together without thinking. If your energy wanes, reach out to your spirit-kin animal partner, or call to the nature spirits who can heal trees and plants and animals *and you*. Sing, whistle, or make feral animal cries as you scatter offerings of natural items to the four directions.

If it feels right, engage key spirits and your spirit-kin animal in deep silent bonding and ask for help in this work. Or maybe commune with a large tree spirit that calls to you. Let their help and loving energy flow through you and out of you in rhythm, or humming, or whistling, or clapping, or rocking, or dancing, or . . . Don't think. Just release your ego self and let the energy flow! As the energy and power build, reach out to whatever force offers help, then slowly turn and face this power and accept it. It may be a particularly powerful rock spirit or a tree spirit. It may be a potent river spirit that is willing to heal one who needs it. Channel whatever positive helpful energy comes to you.

If it feels right to dance with your rattle, then let the magick flow through you as you shake and move. If it feels right to vocalize, then shout and howl and vibrate words or sounds that flow through you. Just let it all flow together in a whirl of movement and sound and light. Then launch the loving comet of your spell to its target. Fall to the earth and release all of this, in silence, in calm nothingness. Feel the nature spirits gather about you, touching and loving you.

When your ritual magick spirals to a slow end, it is time to sit again before the stone tablet altar, thank and honor all the spirits, and sprinkle the remaining offerings in a clockwise circle with appropriate words or sounds of power. Make sure you eat something and drink some pure water; you will need it. Then make a gesture that feels right to you and finally honor and thank your spirit-kin animal, the nature spirits, and the Earth Mother, ending with hands on the altar and vibrating "Maaaaa" three times. Stand and scatter the rest of the animal food clockwise and then, with a final long vibration of "Pa Tan He Ya," begin to walk away in silence. Wander in joy from this wildness, allowing your energized normal human self to slowly rise as your tired animal self slowly sinks back into its peaceful dark home within you. With every step, leave your trance state behind and slowly reenter the mundane world you know. As you do so, give thanks for the wondrous world of nature.

As you silently walk your path home, meditate on the results and the experience. Intuitively feel and see all the interwoven light and energies that filled your spellcraft and all of nature. Drink in the insights that the spirits around you have shared. With every step, honor the Earth Mother and commune with her in silence. Breathe.

As you leave the woods, clap your hands, and vibrate "Ay Aaaa Ta" to close the working. Then reach out your arms and embrace all the light of your spirit self as well as the other lights the spirits have blessed you with. With your hands, bring it all back into your heart center and let it fill your body with energy in silence. It is a lot to absorb! As always, later, record everything you remember about the experience in your journal, including images, symbols, or any words that that relate to the spellcraft you did. They may be lost if you don't record them now.

And remember: When performing feral magick, each experience will be different. Because all things are alive, there is no set way of doing such workings. Reaching out to the world of the nature spirits is always different and unique. Ask any shaman!

PRACTICE

Dream Magick

This rite helps you enter the world of spirits while dreaming or in a deep liminal state. You can do this from the comfort of your own bed or while lying on a couch or camping in the woods. The goal is to enter the dream world and open yourself to the deep unconscious, sometimes called the astral plane. This simple rite is best done as you are drifting in the liminal state between wakefulness and sleep. Astral work like this is best done on or near a full moon.

To perform this practice, all you need is a calm and quiet place where you can lie down and relax without being disturbed, some comfortable clothing like pajamas, two glasses or ceramic cups of pure water, and a small amount of salt. You can also use a small candle (like a tea light) that has no scent, provided it is in a safe ceramic dish and placed away from where you are sleeping. If you are reaching out to a particular spirit-kin animal, place a picture, icon, or image of that spirit-kin animal next to the small candle, perhaps with your intention imprinted on it—for instance, "I will to envision a spirit form orca." If your spirit-kin animal shrine is nearby, all the better. In fact, you can place the candle there. As always, have your journal and a pen within reach.

Get yourself ready to sleep and prepare your bed area. This practice is about working directly with your animal self, so think about the sound that animal makes. If you have a deep connection with your spirit-kin animal partner, get comfortable, and begin to open to it as you will.

When you are ready, sprinkle a bit of salt all around where you will sleep. Visualize a warm circle of light surrounding it. If you like, you can whisper a few words to banish negative energies, like this ancient charm: "Out, out, throughout and about; all good come in, all evil stay out." Place a glass of pure water on each side of your bed somewhere where you will not knock them over. As you do, vibrate "Huuuuuu" and visualize them as full of positive energy and light.

As you sink into bed, concentrate on the image you have in your mind of your spirit-kin animal partner and begin a simple humming sequence to connect with your animal self. Ask it to meet with you in the dreamtime. Then softly utter the appropriate cry of your animal spirit, lie down, and relax.

Breathe deeply to a count of seven for about ten minutes as you focus on the work you want to do. As you move into the liminal state between sleeping and waking, continue this breathing and call to your spirit-kin animal partner, visualizing it clearly as it appears in nature. With every inhalation, see the animal more clearly; with every exhalation, let your vision zoom in on this animal. Once you're able to hold this image, let your mind relax and let this spirit-kin animal image do what it wants to do as you watch it in your imagination. You may silently call it and remind it that you are with it. If it acknowledges this, perfect.

Enjoy watching this important animalistic spirit. Just watch where it goes and what it does. Give your imagination full sway as you slowly fall asleep. Try very hard to remain connected with your feral animal self as you sink into deep sleep. Your deep connection will help you. If you are dozing off and on, honor this spirit-kin animal and focus on your union.

You may wake up several times during the night. If that happens, write down all the dreams, symbols, or images that come to you in your journal. Pay attention to the interactions between you and spirit-kin animal. When you wake up, write down everything. Pour out the glasses of water at the foot of a tree as an offering to thank the Earth Mother and thank the spirit-kin animal. Do this exercise as often as you like to strengthen the bond between your animal self and the spirit-kin animal, your friend.

If you are less than excited about the dreams you receive, do the practice again in a different place or way. It can take several tries. Almost always, doing such work in the wild, even in a tent, brings better results!

Spirit-Kin Animal Feral Group Magick

It is not unusual for a group of Animist devotees and feral folks to gather themselves and their spirit-kin helpers to perform feral magickal work. Gathering, binding, and linking with each other is itself magick, and everyone's spirit-kin animals interacting together is especially exciting. In such nature-spirit-friendly cultures, these group workings are done outside in wildness in a hidden special sacred place. Before it begins, all gathered choose one person to center and lead the ritual.

To begin, all stand in a circle and touch your hearts, then together open arms and unleash your spirit lights. Open arms wider and form a circle with your hands touching. Visualize your open spirit lights forming a powerful and protective circle-sphere as you all vibrate "Huuuuuu" three times to make it so. From that moment on, no human words should be spoken until the clapping begins.

Begin to sway side to side, all moving left and then right together as one while humming the same sequence to call all the nature spirits. As you slide into a trance state, everyone's perceptions will be synchronized as you move slowly into the realm of the spirits and seek to become your feral animal selves. As the trance deepens, each person calls to his or her spirit-kin animal with the appropriate feral cry and all fully enter the Animist world of the others.

Lower your hands and bow to the center and to all the spirits present, vibrating "Ahaaaaa" three times. Then all touch the earth and vibrate "Maaaaa" while communing with the Earth Mother. As one, all stand and open your arms wide to honor the vast green wilderness spirit, and together vibrate "Haaaaaaaa." Then all reach toward the sky and honor the heavens by vibrating the sounds—"Sa" (for the sun), "Ah" (for the moon), and "La" (for the stars/heavens). All are vibrated together as "Ah Sa La." Then all present reach out and touch palms with those on either side, and vibrate "Oooooooo" with love and bonding. Then all touch your chests and bow, honoring all with "Aha!"

Beginning with the chief ritualist and going clockwise, each person voices the appropriate sound of his or her spirit-kin animal; each cry flows through all, with the entire group repeating that spirit's cry loudly. As that spirit fills the circle, all honor it. This takes time, but it is important that each spirit-kin animal be honored in this way.

When all the spirits are then present, all sit in a circle and in silence, with eyes closed or half closed. Begin rocking together, moving forward and back together as the energy of all the spirit-kin animals present gently circles and unites everyone.

The leader now begins a simple humming sequence while all continue to rock gently together as the others join in as they sink deeper into trance. After a time, the humming sequence changes as it flows through all, then another begins to hum a new sequence and communes with his or her spirit-kin animal. Each in turn does this as all pick up the new humming and do as well. This continues until everyone's spirit-kin animal has been honored, until everyone has communed with all the spirits present.

When all have completed the circle, all begin to vibrate "Huuuu" over and over as all raise arms, merging with their own animal spirits. Then the leader vibrates a very long, intense "Huuuuuuuuuu Aha!" and all join in. All touch the earth and go silent, and then sit for a time with the swirling power and what is happening. All is open and calm for a time, all one.

The leader then stands and screams his or her spirit-kin animal's cry, and all leap up and begin to dance, screaming their own spirit-kin animals, cries! Eventually, participants and spirits all dance together, voicing the cries of all present. Rattles, drums, and so on may be used! When the wild madness begins to slow, the leader begins to clap and all join in, coming together, laughing and rejoicing until the sounds fade into silence.

Return to a circle. All again touch palms, chanting "Ah Ha" in deep tones as the trance state recedes and the animal spirits grow calm. Then all raise their arms to center themselves and vibrate "Ah Sa La" to honor the celestial powers. Then all reach out to the side and vibrate "Haaa" to honor the green spirit of the plants and trees. Finally, all place hands on the earth and together vibrate "Maaaa Maaaa Maaaaaa," sending all the excess energies back to the Earth Mother with love. All inhale and receive the power and love of the earth from her in return.

And now it's time to laugh and party and chat and feast. Be sure to compare notes among yourselves and share your magick.

May all be wild and well!

Ah Ha!

CONCLUSION

It is the last days of summer, and I am once again outside lying in my hammock under the massive firs and cedars, which are around 300 years old. Under the swaying boughs I breathe the intoxicating air and am filled with calm as my mind opens to the green. I gently swing and slide into a slight trance and open my animal self. My mind is silent, my senses acute. It is then that I feel and hear the tree spirits that are around me begin to whisper. They are old friends. I now begin to see the energies that flow up the trees from their deep roots, and a glow surrounds me as I slide into the Otherworld. I still my mind, breathe deeply, and expand into the world of the spirits. Without thinking, I perceive the trails of lights and colors as they dance about me. I open deeper into the experience and "see," hear, and feel the young and old spirits now aware of me. They come closer and they swirl about and see me as kin. Some begin to whisper into my mind and soon we begin a varied communion.

This is my feral life, this is the Otherworld where I can embrace the animistic nature spirits and powers of nature. As a fairly erudite author, Tantric, Thelemite, Witch, and much more in my long life, I lie under the trees and let go of much of the complex rituals and creeds. The ancient grimoires and rote practices which do work for many just aren't so necessary for me anymore. I am left with my wolf spirit friend and my own animal self for the most part; and so it has been this way for me for several years as it has been for so many ancient peoples and sacred gurus who always end up showing us the key of "nothing doing nothing." As a Westerner, except for four glorious years in Japan, this process has meant gently letting go of most everything occult that is ponderous, intellectual, or cultural, though I honor them. I have more fully embraced the crucial reality of an intelligent, conscious Earth and the ever-present, interested, and communicative spirits of nature in the wildness. This includes my spirit-kin animal wolf who is ever guiding, protecting, and padding about me. He is part of me and I him, as has become clear every full moon! I've never had so much fun.

Once I let go of all my studious cultural baggage, I never looked back, and the spirits were waiting for me in the greenery. In my yard as a child, I knew yet forgot everything I know now—all things are alive. This was continually taught to me in magickal moments in the Cascade Mountains, in the shrines of Japan, and in the temples and gatherings in Thailand, Cambodia, Nepal, India, Guatemala, Mexico, and so many other glowing places where the spirits and shamans found and showed me the powers and spirits. Here, now, in my little woods next to my house, I lie in my hammock, and it all comes to me. The spirits are everywhere, and all is alive; I have but to open my animal self and be really, truly aware. And there I am, in the Other amidst the spirits and the astounding, colorful, active web of Nature.

This is the animistic world ancient hominids experienced and worked with for hundreds of thousands of years. It is clear to see in the cave paintings, archeological digs, and in the still-existing animistic cultures all over the world. They desperately seek to save the forests and the spirits, and this, too, is work we need to support.

Today, most of us are wrapped in layers of abstracts, floods of internet information, destructive culture, rigid beliefs, and so much blindness, sadness, and damage. We mostly don't live within the potency of nature, we just kind of visit it—and often damage it, and almost never pay attention to it. We all know that this is not healthy.

Letting go of the blinders and cell phones within *real wilderness* is like tearing off a blindfold. With some work, you will emerge from your cultural cocoon and experience the truth: **Everything is alive.** And more: **You are part of this!** The living powers surround you and can mentor, help, and heal you. You have but to open to the feral magick of the spirits.

The real green world has always been waiting for you. Everything about feral magick and Neo-Animism is about nature. Everything.

I have become more feral as I am more deeply with the Earth. I have become aware that "the most open and useful magick" means working with the most ancient of helper spirits and powers within nature. It is a narrow path we human animals must walk in this chaotic world. Our way forward is to listen, accept, learn from, and be guided by the powers and spirits of animals and nature, as people have done for hundreds of thousands of years in harmony with nature. We are continually offered the flowing, living spiritual energy, the plants, animals, waters, and all things of the earth which we have ignored but desperately need. Time to wake up our animal self and tear the blinders off.

My experience has been that we alter reality through narrow ego and cultural indoctrination, but nature can help us alter our perceptions and our reality framework by revealing to us that *everything truly experienced is not what was taught to us.* As so many tribal people have told me, nature teaches us everything of importance; if we part the veil of cultural ignorance, we can see that everything in the natural world is an astounding, miraculous wonder. It is time to put down the cell phones, unhook, think openly, and awaken to the very real world of infinite wildness, life, and astounding spirits and powers.

The Earth Mother and all the nature spirits have been harmed and ignored, but in the wildness, they abide and await our return to sanity. A primal feral wave is rising among people now, maybe in your group. Many people are awakening to the stupid environmental suicide we are creating for ourselves out of greed and blindness. More and more people seek ways to step back from the ongoing planetary destruction. Saving deep, healthy nature and its spirit guardians is, I believe, where our revival and spiritual awakening await. When you accept that you are and have always been an animal, then you can open to your animal self and open to the Otherworld that is real and crucial and seeks you to help save our world. **When you enter the Other, you will be home in the truest sense.**

With an open heart and a howl, I call on you to truly embrace and embody the wildness, all the nature and animal spirits, and the utter bliss of letting nature embrace and become part of you. Never ever forget: **Everything is alive.** Live it.

Ever and always—be wild and well!

BIBLIOGRAPHY

AtHope, Damien. *damienmarieathope.com*.

Behnia, Rudy. *zuckermaninstitute.columbia.edu*.

Eliade, Mircea. (1964). *Shamanism: Archaic Techniques of Ecstasy*. Princeton University Press.

Guirand, F. (ed.). (1987). *New Larousse Encyclopedia of Mythology*. Crescent Books.

Harvey, G. (2005). *Animism: Respecting the Living World*. Columbia University Press.

Hutton, R. (2007). *Shamans: Siberian Spirituality and the Western Imagination*. Bloomsbury Publishing PLC.

Illes, Judika. (2009). *The Encyclopedia of Spirits*. HarperCollins.

Insoll, T. (2020). "Animism and Totemism," in *The Oxford Handbook of the Archaeology of Ritual & Religion*. Oxford University Press. doi.org/10.1093/oxfordhb/9780199232444.013.0063.

Kennedy, K. W. S. (1914). *Animism*. (2nd ed.). Office of "The Lay reader."

Lupa. (2016). *Nature Spirituality from the Ground Up: Connect with Totems in Your Ecosystem*. Llewellyn Publications.

———. (2022). *DIY Animism: Your Personal Guide to Animal Spirits.* Independently published.

MIT. "Primitive Brain Is 'Smarter' than We Think," *Science Daily*, sciencedaily.com.

Narby, J. (ed.). (2001). *Shamans through Time.* Thames & Hudson Ltd.

Nida, E. A. (1959). *Introducing Animism.* Friendship Press.

Sagan, C. (1983). *Cosmos.* Little Brown Book Group Limited.

Sargent, D. (1993). *Global Ritualism: Myth and Magic around the World.* Llewellyn Publications.

———. (2017). *Naga Magick: The Wisdom of the Serpent Lords.* Original Falcon Press, LLC.

———. (2020). *Werewolf Magick: Authentic Practical Lycanthropy.* Llewellyn Publications.

———. (2022). *Werewolf Pack Magick: A Shapeshifter's Book of Shadows.* Llewellyn Publications.

VanPool, Christine S., and Elizabeth Newsome. "The Spirit in the Material: A Case Study of Animism in the American Southwest," *www.jstor.org*.

Walker, B. G. (1995). *The Woman's Dictionary of Symbols and Sacred Objects.* Castle Books.

———. (1995). *The Woman's Encyclopedia of Myths and Secrets.* HarperCollins.

Wilson, R. A. (1983). *Prometheus Rising.* Falcon Press.

World Flutelore. "Folktales, Myths, and Other Stories of Magical Flute Power," *academic.oup.com*.

ABOUT THE AUTHOR

Denny Sargent is an artist and university instructor in linguistics and Teaching English to Speakers of Other Languages (TESOL). Sargent's many extensive global travels and esoteric studies have informed his books. Involved in a number of esoteric traditions and orders for decades, he has written about alternative religions, hermetic magick, Taoism, animism, Shinto, and Tantra. His published books include *Your Guardian Angel and You*, *Werewolf Magick*, *Clean Sweep*, and *Naga Magick*. He lives in Seattle, Washington. Find him at *dennysargentauthor.com*.

TO OUR READERS

Weiser Books, an imprint of Red Wheel/Weiser, publishes books across the entire spectrum of occult, esoteric, speculative, and New Age subjects. Our mission is to publish quality books that will make a difference in people's lives without advocating any one particular path or field of study. We value the integrity, originality, and depth of knowledge of our authors.

Our readers are our most important resource, and we appreciate your input, suggestions, and ideas about what you would like to see published.

Visit our website at *www.redwheelweiser.com*, where you can learn about our upcoming books and free downloads, and also find links to sign up for our newsletter and exclusive offers.

You can also contact us at *info@rwwbooks.com* or at

Red Wheel/Weiser, LLC
65 Parker Street, Suite 7
Newburyport, MA 01950